C000132870

▶ The Manipulation of Online Self-Presentation

DOI: 10.1057/9781137483416.0001

Palgrave Studies in Cyberpsychology

Series Editor: Jens Binder, Nottingham Trent University, UK

Titles include:

John Waterworth and Giuseppe Riva
FEELING PRESENT IN THE PHYSICAL WORLD AND COMPUTER MEDIATED
ENVIRONMENTS

Sandy Schumann
HOW THE INTERNET SHAPES COLLECTIVE ACTIONS

Christian Happ and Andre Melzer
EMPATHY AND VIOLENT VIDEO GAMES

Daria Kuss and Mark Griffiths
INTERNET ADDICTION IN PSYCHOTHERAPY

Alison Attrill
THE MANIPULATION OF ONLINE SELF-PRESENTATION
Create, Edit, Re-edit and Present

Palgrave Studies in Cyberpsychology
Series Standing Order ISBN 978-1-137-44948-1 (Hardback)
(outside North America only)

You can receive future titles in this series as they are published by placing a standing order. Please contact your bookseller or, in case of difficulty, write to us at the address below with your name and address, the title of the series and the ISBN quoted above.

Customer Services Department, Macmillan Distribution Ltd, Houndmills, Basingstoke, Hampshire RG21 6XS, England

DOI: 10.1057/9781137483416.0001

palgrave▸pivot

The Manipulation of Online Self-Presentation: Create, Edit, Re-edit and Present

Alison Attrill
University of Wolverhampton, UK

palgrave
macmillan

DOI: 10.1057/9781137483416.0001

First published 2015 by
PALGRAVE MACMILLAN

Palgrave Macmillan in the UK is an imprint of Macmillan Publishers Limited, registered in England, company number 785998, of Houndmills, Basingstoke, Hampshire RG21 6XS.

Palgrave Macmillan in the US is a division of St Martin's Press LLC, 175 Fifth Avenue, New York, NY 10010.

Palgrave Macmillan is the global academic imprint of the above companies and has companies and representatives throughout the world.

Palgrave® and Macmillan® are registered trademarks in the United States, the United Kingdom, Europe and other countries.

ISBN: 978–1–137–48342–3   EPUB
ISBN: 978–1–137–48341–6   PDF
ISBN: 978–1–137–48340–9   Hardback

A catalogue record for this book is available from the British Library.

A catalog record for this book is available from the Library of Congress.

www.palgrave.com/pivot

DOI: 10.1057/9781137483416

For my favourite big person, my favourite little person and my favourite dog! Thank you for all of your love and support.

DOI: 10.1057/9781137483416.0001

Contents

DOI: 10.1057/9781137483416.0001

DOI: 10.1057/9781137483416.0001

Glossary

acceptance-seeking: a motive used to create a sense of belonging by engaging in online behaviours.

acquisitive self-presentation: used to gain approval from others through positive presentation of the self.

actual self: the self a person really is at a given time in a given situation (see also *true self, real self* and *core self*).

allocentric individuals: group-focused individuals.

▶ *alter-self:* representation of a completely different and unrepresentative version of the real self.

asynchronous communication: exchanges that have delayed responses in lapsed time.

belonging: the need to feel connected to other human beings.

Big Five Personality Factors: overarching categories of traits, for example, *openness, conscientiousness, extraversion, agreeableness and neuroticism,* that are characterised by personality markers.

blog: online, ongoing written report pertaining to one's life or a specific topic.

body image: subjective perceptions and feelings about the self looks to others.

bonding relationships: strong ties, often found in close emotional relationships; usually with family and close friends (see also *strong bonds*).

DOI: 10.1057/9781137483416.0002

breadth: the broadness of the self-information shared with others.

bridging relationships: weak ties, often found in larger social networks, often among a larger group of friends, or those who have similar goals/interests (see also *weak bonds*).

collectivist societies: individuals are focused on the group.

computer-mediated communication: form of communication carried out via technological devices.

coping mechanism: aids to processing information in a way that aids one's own positive sense of self and well-being.

core self: the self a person really is at a given time in a given situation (see also *true self, real self* and *actual self*).

courtly love: the way in which people used to engage in dating in the 1800s.

cyber-flirting: flirtatious exchanges that take place online.

cybernetics: understanding systems and structures that can be operationalised and controlled.

cyberpsychology: role of psychology factors in all forms of technology-human interaction behaviours, interactions and communications.

cyberself: the self that a person presents online (see also *digital self*).

depression: feeling of low mood, lethargy and unwillingness to engage in social interaction.

depth: the level of personal and intimate self-information shared with others.

digital self: the self that a person presents online (see also *cyberself*).

e-health: the overarching term given to all health-related online activities.

email etiquette: the rules associated with the tone and grammar used in email.

emotional distance: the discrepancy in how people feel about a given situation.

FaceTime: video-communication tool that enables synchronous communication.

DOI: 10.1057/9781137483416.0002

fantasy self: a pretend or imagined self that cannot be presented offline.

friendships: relationships that exist between people who share similar interests or who share some level of social interaction (see also *platonic relationships*).

FtF: face-to-face

human belongingness: humans have the fundamental and basic need to create significant and lasting relationships in a way that makes them feel wanted, liked and connected to other humans.

Human-Computer Interaction: study of actual interactions that humans have with any form of technology.

hyperpersonal: online interactions become more important to the individual than their offline relationships and interactions.

ideal self: the self a person strives to be.

identity: the person who the self represents. Created from social and individual norms of behaviour. How a person represents themselves.

idiocentric individuals: individually focused individuals.

impression management: way in which people try to manage others' perceptions and interpretations of the self in order to see them in a positive light (see also *self-presentation*).

independent self-construals: focus on internal, private aspects of self as distinct from the environment and social contexts.

individualistic societies: individuals are focused on the self.

information-seeking: the act of looking for information either online or offline.

interdependent self-construals: focus on external, public aspects of self intertwined with the environment and social contexts.

Internet: globally accessible world wide web.

internet: term specific to cyberpsychology. Localised network to which a select number of people have access (see also *intranet*)

Internet arena: different types of websites that come together under umbrella terms such as dating websites, social media websites and e-commerce websites.

intranet: localised network to which a select number of people have access (see also *internet*).

involuntary self-disclosure: needs-must sharing of information to achieve a desired goal.

loneliness: feeling experienced in the absence of social interaction.

moral reasoning: decision about right or wrong action to take in a given situation.

morals: messages about behaviour that are often conveyed through tales and stories.

multiple audience: information presented online may be perceived by a number of different people.

naïve psychologist: the human being is a lay psychologist who attempts to piece together overt and covert clues to understand their own and others' behaviour.

offline: behaviours, interactions and communications carried out without any use of technology.

online: behaviours, interactions and communications carried out through use of an Internet, internet or intranet.

online self: the person that people present as themselves online.

online world: any space, webpage, website or other form of interactive forum on the Internet.

ought self: the self a person believes they need to be based on other peoples' norms, standards and expectations.

para-authentic self: representation of the real or actual self online.

personality: characteristics that provide a person with consistency in their behaviours across times and situations, which also make people similar yet unique.

personality markers: different traits that come together to create a person's personality along certain dimensions (see also *Big Five Personality Factors*).

perverse social capital: interactions that result in negative social benefits.

DOI: 10.1057/9781137483416.0002

physical distance: actual tangible distance between people.

platonic relationships: relationships that exist between people who share similar interests or who share some level of social interaction (see also *friendships*).

poster: person putting information online (see also *presenter*).

presenter: person putting information online (see also *poster*).

prevention strategies: result from sense of duty or obligation; employed to avoid negative outcomes.

privacy concern: concerns about the level of privacy of one's online information and exchanges.

productive social capital: interactions that reap positive social benefits.

promiscuous friending: low boundaries are applied of befriending people online, often by adding people as friends to a social networking profile when they are complete strangers, with the aim of inflating their audience size.

promotion strategies: based on hopes and/or aspirations employed specifically to evoke a positive outcome.

protective self-presentation: used to avoid approval from others through use of neutral and modest presentation of the self.

psychology: study of the mind and behaviour.

real self: the self a person really is at a given time in a given situation (see also *true self, actual self* and *core self*).

recipient: the person who is expected to receive or perceive information shared online (see also *target*).

romantic relationships: relationships that usually exist between two loving individuals. Implies a physical relationship.

Second Life: an online virtual environment.

self identity: one's construct of one's own image and understanding of their self.

self-actualisation: process of working towards an ideal or acceptable self.

DOI: 10.1057/9781137483416.0002

self-concealment: people actively suppress negative personal information to promote a positive self-image.

self-concept: individual's overall notion of the self.

self-concept clarity: overall positive self that is free of psychological distress or discrepancy among different selves.

self-disclosure: process of sharing self-information with others.

self-efficacy: one's own perceived ability to complete a task.

self-esteem: perceived positive or negative evaluation of the self.

self-guides: internal standards against which a person compares their thoughts and actions for meaning and value.

self-knowledge: autobiographical information that influences how a person perceives, interprets and responds to overt and covert behaviours.

self-presentation: the monitoring and presentation of a carefully crafted view of oneself in order to create a certain image (see also *impression management*).

shy: physical and psychological discomfort, awkwardness and apprehension when around other people.

Skype: video-communication tool that enables synchronous communication.

social anxiety: feeling of psychological distress in social situations.

social capital: the sense of social bonding that helps relationships exist both online and offline.

social compensation: seeking out of activities online to fulfil human desires and needs not fulfilled in offline interactions.

social cues: situational factors that evoke or influence a person's behaviour through the information that they convey.

social enhancement: online behaviours extend and benefit offline activities, desires and needs.

social media: umbrella term used to categorise social interactive media online such as Facebook, Twitter and Instagram.

social network: different social groups to which one belongs.

DOI: 10.1057/9781137483416.0002

social network analysis: analysis of the networks in which one engages.

social networking sites: online social groups to which one belongs.

social norms: the social rules and regulations of a society.

social roles: the roles which a person carries out in their daily lives, such as that of mother, father, sister or brother.

strong bonds: interactions that have strong consequences for the existence of a relationship and importance to the individual.

synchronous communication: exchanges that occur in real time with immediate responses.

target: the person who is expected to receive or perceive information shared online (see also *recipient*).

temporal distance: differences in time.

true self: the self a person really is at a given time in a given situation (see also *actual self*, *real self* and *core self*).

trust verification: seeking out online information to ascertain that a person is who they say they are online.

virtual environments: a space for social interaction created in cyberspace (see also *virtual worlds*).

virtual worlds: a space for social interaction created in cyberspace (see also *virtual environments*).

voluntary self-disclosure: information freely shared with others.

warranting: cue that can be used to verify someone's online self as an accurate extension or representation of their offline self.

warranting principle: evaluation that occurs when someone is judging online information as an accurate representation of another person.

warranting value: the degree to which offline self-information matches the information a person shares online.

weak bonds: interactions that are of no consequence or importance to the individual.

DOI: 10.1057/9781137483416.0002

1
Introduction – Who Am I?

Abstract: *Providing an introduction, this chapter outlines the main concepts that build the foundation of the book. It considers the reasons as to why we need to understand the different selves that people present on diverse websites across the Internet. In doing so, it also looks at the ways in which the Internet is constantly evolving, and how people use this to their advantage in ways that extend and enhance their offline self-presentations online.*

Key words: cyberself; Internet landscapes; Internet tools; online self

Attrill, Alison. *The Manipulation of Online Self-Presentation: Create, Edit, Re-edit and Present.* Basingstoke: Palgrave Macmillan, 2015. DOI: 10.1057/9781137483416.0003.

On welcoming you to this text on how we create and represent ourselves online, the easiest way to start the discussion around how we create versions of the self that we then use on the Internet is to have you ask yourself the question *"Who am I?"*. You may have asked yourself this question on numerous occasions relating to many different activities, relationships and across diverse social settings. It is the question of who we believe our core central guiding self to be, as well as how we believe ourselves to change depending upon factors such as time, situation and people with whom we are interacting. Mostly, we consider and ponder who we are when thinking about our offline selves and our offline interactions. At this point, let us denote *offline* as any behaviours or interactions that we carry out without any use of technology, including mobile phones, gaming consoles or smart TVs. All *online* behaviours are those carried out on any interconnected network that enables connecting to and interacting with people and other devices via a technological device. Such behaviours can include, but are not limited to, emailing, instant messaging, blogging, social networking, shopping, banking and gaming.

Of interest for the current text is how we represent ourselves online across these and many other different types of online behaviours. Returning to the *"Who am I?"* question, understanding who we think we are, who we believe our core selves to be becomes a rather more difficult question when we throw the Internet into the mix. Some might believe that they behave entirely differently online and offline. Others might perceive their online self to be a real representation of their offline self. Many individuals might think that how they present themselves online has little or no consequences to both their online and offline interactions, relationships and existences. This text outlines the theories and research associated with some of these considerations. In particular, it focuses on how humans behave online, how they create similar or distinct versions of self online compared to offline, and the possible consequences of these self-portrayals. In doing so, it explores whether the *online self* is the same as the offline self, an entirely different entity to the offline self, or an extension of the offline self. It focuses heavily on *identity*, how individuals create their self-identities, how they are constructed and manipulated to fit temporal and situational norms or behavioural requirements. Bearing this in mind, it is important to note that identity online can be understood in at least two ways. It can imply how one creates and represents the self online. It can also mean how one's identity is revealed online by the self, other users and/or services, people to whom

DOI: 10.1057/9781137483416.0003

we have entrusted our information which they subsequently pass on to others. This text focuses more on the former, whereas the latter is more relevant to privacy and trust concerns relation to online behaviour. A further note is made to the use of *our selves* or *our self* as distinct words in this text. These words have different connotations to the use of *ourselves* or *ourself* with the former denoting the *self* as a distinct entity.

Before jumping straight in with these topics, it is important to first note that this text is not intended as a comprehensive literature review of all of the areas outlined. Rather, it reflects a starting point for anyone who is interested in any of these areas of how people present their selves online. There are a number of instances where information may be repeated throughout the text as it is relevant to different areas of consideration. This repetition was believed to be important to the flow and understanding of the material. Cross references have been included where possible between chapters and sections to help the reader follow the flow of the material and some of the arguments and statements made throughout.

At this point, you might also have noticed that the word *Internet* has been capitalised. In *Cyberpsychology*, the globally accessible World Wide Web is referred to as the Internet. An *internet*, identified with a small "i" is a localised network to which a select number of people have access. In other disciplines this might also be known as an *intranet*. The focus of this text is on the self as presented and represented via the Internet rather than localised internets. This can now be accessed via a multitude of devices, from personal computers to mobile phones, and from gaming consoles to smart televisions. The Internet is there. It is not going away and much of human life now assumes that we all have access to it and are able to competently use it. Although there is an ongoing debate about who uses the Internet, how and for what, the focus of this text is on how we construct our selves online. It is therefore beyond the confines of this work to discuss, for example, the existence of a digital generation in Internet use. The reader is referred to the recent book *Cyberpsychology* by Attrill (2015) for discussions around these and many more factors that also play a role in shaping online behaviours. Just before moving on to consider why we need to explore the ways in which people edit and possibly recreate different versions of self online, some of the key concepts that will be core to the understanding of this text will be briefly outlined, beginning with a description of the area of study that has become known as Cyberpsychology.

DOI: 10.1057/9781137483416.0003

1.1   Cyberpsychology

The word *cyberpsychology* is derived from the words *cybernetics* and *psychology*. The former refers to understanding systems and structures that can be operationalised and controlled, while the word psychology is most synonymous with the understanding of the interaction of the mind and behaviour. Cyberpsychology is a rapidly growing and ever-evolving sub-discipline of psychology that explores the underlying psychological processes, motivations, intentions, behavioural outcomes and effects of online behaviour on both our online and offline lives. It focuses on how the mind and body evoke and react to interactions with other human beings and services via technology. This is not the same as the study of *human-computer interaction*. This focuses more on the actual interactions that humans have with any form of technology with a view to designing new technologies and enhance existing technologies. As you might imagine, the rapidity with which online behaviours are growing, and how people are now using different types of services online for a variety of reasons, causes quite a difficulty for researchers being able to keep up with the ever-changing landscape of the Internet. There might be times throughout this text where what might appear to be older research is cited. Other times, work that has considered offline behaviours might be applied to understanding online equivalents. This is not only a sign of the need for much more research in the area of cyberpsychology, but also of the need to consider the Internet as an ever-evolving tool for human behaviour. We will return to these notions throughout the text, but for now it shall be noted that the use of older or offline research in certain places in the book serves to illustrate certain points or underline arguments. Most of these will revolve around the core concept of the book that is the "*self*".

1.2   Online and offline selves

> A major shift is occurring in which digital machines are beginning to adapt to humans. Through the refinements of eye-tracking, voice, and gesture control, the distinction between the physical and the digital self will no longer have an interface barrier. (Pak, 2014, p. 141)

If you are asked "who are you", what are the first ten things that spring to mind? You could respond with your gender, age and nationality. You might

DOI: 10.1057/9781137483416.0003

say, mother, father, sister, brother, daughter, son, lecturer, shop assistant or factory worker. You might reply that you are a student, that you like a certain type of sport, or that you prefer reading and playing computer games. Alternatively, you might focus on your attributes and describe yourself as a kind, well-rounded human being who likes to engage in charity work. Whatever your reply, you would be providing information about yourself that enables another person to build a picture of who you are, a sense of your *self*. All of the adjectives and nouns that you use to reply to the question of who you are reflect words that you use to create your own *self identity*. This is how you construct your own image and understanding of yourself. It is also how you want others to see you. You might hold a version of your self that you believe to be an absolute true reflection of who you really are, the parts of you that are consistent regardless of time or situation, or those people with whom you are interacting. This *core self* is however malleable. Sometimes, you might change your behaviour to suit the people you are with, or the situation in which you find yourself. To illustrate this point, consider your own behaviour across different situations. You would likely behave differently on a first date to how you would behave if you were out for a celebration with your closest friends. This shows a malleable aspect to the self. You can change your current self to suit the environment and any given situation in which you find yourself in much the same way as you may change your clothes or outfit to suit a situation. This occurs without distracting from the notion of a core self that remains situationally and temporally stable and consistent. We also use our knowledge about ourselves to assess, interpret and respond to other people. Think about the last time that you were in a restaurant. If you took a look around you at the other diners, you probably made assumptions about them based on their appearance and the *social cues* that they were using, such as facial expressions and body language. Your interpretation of these factors would have been influenced by how you think you should behave in that situation. Your *self-knowledge* thus guides how you construct your self, how you change and manipulate aspects of your character and behaviour depending upon a number of factors, and how you interpret others' behaviour based on your own notion of self. Your self-knowledge is therefore probably one of the most powerful cognitive tools that you possess. Not only does it analyse yours' and others' behaviours along with situational cues, but it also places cognitive interpretation and responses on those behaviours. In other words, how you think and feel, your emotions and your overall sense of well-being are all somehow related to and

DOI: 10.1057/9781137483416.0003

guided by your own self-knowledge. We are most often at the forefront of our actions and experience these from our own perspective, based on our own personal experiences and judgements.

There will be a number of points in the text in which the role of cognitions and cognitive processes in online self-representations and behaviours will be considered. To do so, interpretations of memory storage systems and processes from both cognitive and social psychological theories will be used (see Chapter 5). For the purpose of this introductory chapter however, let us consider the self as a flexible malleable construct that is influenced and guided by one's own and others' perceptions and interpretations of a range of external factors in the offline world. This brief definition of self focuses largely on the offline self. In response to the question of who you are, you would unlikely respond with aspects of your *digital self*, or *cyberself*, and yet for most inhabitants of westernised cultures, the Internet has become an integral part of daily living. Both of these terms are used to refer to the self that you present when engaging in any online activity. Although you can represent yourself digitally across a number of digitalised media, from virtual world technology to mobile phone apps, throughout the current work we will refer to the cyberself, online self or digital self as being the person you are online, regardless of the technology used to access the online world. Where the word *self* occurs, it is used to denote who you are offline.

1.3   Self-presentation and impression management

As the title of this book suggests, people are able to present themselves online in any way they choose to. This is a process of *self-presentation*, which has been described by Leary (1995, p. 2) as "the process of controlling how one is perceived by other people". Self-presentation occurs when people carefully monitor, manage and present the self in a certain way with the intention to maintain a certain image of oneself to another person(s) (Brown, 2007). This manipulated presentation in turn affects how people create their own image of themselves (Harter, 1998; Subrahmanyam & Greenfield, 2008). Many factors influence how people present themselves to others, including the roles that they play in life along with the rules and regulations of the society within which they exist. There are many ways in which one's identity, self-image and self-presentation come together to create an overall sense of self. Having

DOI: 10.1057/9781137483416.0003

a positive sense of self is very much linked to our psychological well-being (see e.g., Berzonsky, 2003a, 2003b; Luyckx, Schwartz, Goossens, Soenens & Beyers, 2008; Marcia, 1993; Meeus, 1996; Meeus, Iedema, Helsen & Vollebergh, 1999). It is therefore not surprising that we engage in *impression management*, that is the way in which we try to manage others' perceptions and interpretations of our self in order that they see us in a positive light. Online, we can do this in a number of ways, from extending a true representation of who we are offline to our online activities to creating a completely different persona that provides us with a false sense of anonymity. It is worth noting that often the terms self-presentation and impression management are used interchangeably, both implying how we construct and represent the self to evoke a certain impression about us from others.

One of the questions that will be considered throughout this book is that of why we engage in impression management online. If you consider your own online interactions on popular websites such as Facebook, then you might post different content depending upon what you want to achieve from the post. It might simply be that you want to create a feeling of being liked or accepted by other people liking your post. Another reason might be that you experience a positive reward from the responses to your posts, from presenting certain aspects of your self, or presenting a certain version of yourself online (e.g., Leary & Allen, 2011). There are a multitude of reasons as to why people behave the way they do relating to the online self-presentations. Many of these will be explored in this text as will the notion of just how free we are to play around with the editing and presentation of our cyberselves. Some might argue that we have a lot more freedom online than offline to present ourselves any way we choose to, but that may not be the case for all types of online interactions. If playing an online game, for instance, a player might use a nickname, but if engaging in online dating with the real intent of finding a romantic partner, hiding or manipulating aspects of their self-presentation in order to appear in a more favourable light may not be the best way to create an impression that results in any long-lasting offline interaction.

1.4   Ever-changing landscapes

Throughout this book, one of the underlying themes is the notion that most work carried out with the ambition of understanding online

DOI: 10.1057/9781137483416.0003

representations of self and associated behaviours is characterised by the absence of consideration for the wide and varied landscape that is the Internet. In our offline world, we attend different places and venues, meet with different groups of people and carry out a range of private and social activities throughout our lives, many with direct goals in mind, some with just an ambling social flare to them. Some events will be short-lived, others will be longer and have a more meaningful impact on our lives.

In the psychology of offline behaviour, there are a number of sub-disciplines that are utilised to understand diverse interactions. Indeed, there are theories that aim to explain our existence before we actually take our first breath in the world, theories that track our psychological processes, progress, developments and demise from birth to death, theories that explain the impact of adolescence on our social and personal lives, theories that explain how and why we do the jobs we do, the sports we engage in, why some people are more lonely, socially anxious, clinically depressed or more extravert, agreeable and open than others, as well as theories that attempt to categories us according to personalities and stereotypes, to name just some of the areas that offline psychology aims to conceptualise, theorise and explain. In its infancy, cyberpsychology appeared to ignore most of these areas in favour of a somewhat biased view towards applying social, social cognitive and personality theories to understanding online behaviour. This application occurred irrespective of the online behaviour being explained and was likely an artefact of the notion that most of the actions engaged in online are of a social nature, such as the conversing via email, instant messenger, chat rooms, Skype and social networking sites. This focus could be somewhat forgiven, especially since it stages the Internet as a playground in which people explore and present their self in a multitude of ways. Indeed, much of the early online behaviours that were studied were very much of a social nature: gaming, relationship building, dating, chat rooms, discussion boards and information seeking, all behaviours and interactions that require some level of impression management online. More recently, the Internet has evolved into an arena for all aspects of our financial transactions, from shopping to banking to gambling. A lot of activities that were traditionally carried out offline have moved online, even booking appointments to visit one's doctor or health advisor.

With a multitude of behaviours thus emerging as regular online behaviours, there is a need for the literature to consider how the self

DOI: 10.1057/9781137483416.0003

engages in these varied activities and how it may be represented in a diverse and varied manner depending upon the actual behaviour or interaction engaged in. For instance, if you are replying to an email about a job vacancy, you present yourself very differently to how you might self-present were you corresponding with your best friend about your night out at the weekend. Both communications carry aspects of online self-representation, which will likely differ depending upon the online action engaged in. Throughout this text, the aim is to bear this diversity in mind. The Internet is as wide and varied as our offline lives. We have lots of different theories to explain all of these facets of offline activity. The task now is to evolve theories that can equally explain the diversity of online self-representations and behaviours according to Internet arena, goals and activities of the user.

That said, we should also bear in mind at this point that some self-representations may not necessarily be associated with different Internet arenas, but with just being online. Some people might claim that they are who they are wherever they are, whom-ever they are with and whatever they are doing, regardless of whether this is online or offline. They might tell you that they are always their *true* or *real* self, regardless of temporal or situational factors. Psychologists, on the other hand, might suggest this not to be the case. A number of people now suggest online selves to reflect either the *ideal* or *ought* self, or even a *fantasy self* that simply cannot be expressed offline. In Chapter 2, we will explore these different types of self in far more detail before looking at the interplay of *personality factors* and self-representation online in Chapter 3.

1.5   The physical Internet

There is often a tendency for researchers to talk about an *online world* and a *real world*, with the latter referring to individuals' offline lives. By calling the offline world, the real world, a connotation is evoked of online activity being less real. However, the Internet has very much become a real component of many peoples' everyday lives. To them, it is no less real than the offline world. This text therefore distinguishes between offline and online worlds, and not between online and real worlds with the online world being considered to be equally as real and valid to its users as the offline world. It has often been argued that events, objects, items and people are only as real as their physical presence. However, if

DOI: 10.1057/9781137483416.0003

we demonstrate throughout this text that peoples' experiences online can affect how they construct both their online and offline selves, and impact not only upon their perceptions but also on their behaviour both online and offline, it can be feasibly assumed that the actions of the cyberself are just as *real* as any offline interactions.

Reports and interpretations of how real peoples' worlds are to them and how they manipulate their self-presentation often cite the sociologist Erving Goffman (1922–1982) as providing a basis for understanding humans' impression management. No text on the self would be complete without considering Goffman's Theory of Self-Presentation (1959) from the then ground-breaking text entitled *The Presentation of Self in Everyday Life* (1959). Taking lead from Shakespeare's *As You Like It*, Goffman later wrote that "presumably the telephone and mails provide reduced versions of the primordial real thing" (1983, p. 2) implying an inferiority of telephone communication over face-to-face interactions at that time. Human beings are adaptive. According to Goffman, humans create their own self-image which they subsequently present to others on the stage that is life. All human actions and interactions are thus nothing other than actors playing out the roles of everyday life. We manipulate and consciously control these actions to present ourselves in a controlled manner. Moreover, other people interpret and react to our manipulated self-presentations. In turn, we respond to those interpretations and reactions, creating the world as an interactive stage, with individuals and groups working singularly and together to create and shape impressions of one another. We adapt to our ever-changing environments, creating new ways to communicate and stage our lives by engaging with other people near and far. Meyrowitz (1989) once noted that ever-changing modes of communication bring with them the increasing opportunity for creating different variations of the self, selves that respond to the situation, or world, in which the self is interacting. Although offering a nod to the role of emerging technologies in his statement about the telephone, Goffman's theory was very much of a time in which technology as we now know it was nothing other than a figment of science fiction writers' imaginations. It was based very much on notions of a real physical presence between communicators, or actors. Nonetheless, this notion of the self illustrates (1) the malleability of the self depending upon a situation and interaction partner(s), and (2) that humans are adaptable to the situations in which they find themselves and the tools they have at hand. To experience an interaction as real, we might assume that people

DOI: 10.1057/9781137483416.0003

need to be physically present. Recent theories suggest that physicality is irrelevant and that this presence can be created in cyberspace through three main features: *personal* (a person feels that s/he actually physically present), *environmental* (the surroundings respond to the person) and *social* (other people are present in the environment) (Heeter, 1992). This would suggest that as long as these three factors can be satisfied, a person may feel as if s/he is having a real and valid interaction, irrespective of whether there is physical or face-to-face contact. As demonstrated throughout the following chapters, people may thus use many different self-representations online that constitute real and valid experiences, mostly because they are somehow representing a version of self that interacts with other people online in a shared cyber-environment in a way that may evoke a sense of social interaction.

1.6   The Internet tool

You may be familiar with the colloquialism "guns don't kill people, people do". It suggests that a person is always responsible for his/her own actions, and that the gun is the tool used to carry out an action or behaviour. In this section, the notion is explored that the Internet is nothing other than a tool that people use to shape and carry out their own behaviours in a motivated goal-directed manner. As already mentioned people carry out many diverse activities across many different types of *Internet arena*. For the purposes of this book, we will define Internet arenas as different types of websites. For example, social networking sites fall under the cluster of social media as do Twitter and Instagram. Online banking and shopping fall under the rubric of e-commerce while the NHS information service website and any other health support services online fall under the arena of eHealth. The reason as to how and why people use these different Internet arenas is as wide and varied as the number of different types of Internet website available. Human beings have always used tools for their behaviours. They are nothing if not adaptors and creators of tool use. There is some now famous research in the area of Social Psychology that illustrated this point nicely in terms of social behaviour. Berkowitz and LePage (1967) carried out experiments to measure participants' levels of perceived aggression in the presence of various social cues. When these cues were sporting equipment such as a shuttlecock, participants reported feeling far less angry than when

DOI: 10.1057/9781137483416.0003

in the presence of a gun. This offered a turning point for psychology to perceive humans as interactors with their environments, and those environments offering cues and stimuli that create certain thoughts and feelings in humans which could lead to a given action. Now, while the participants may have experienced higher levels of aggression in the presence of a weapon, the weapon itself did not create that feeling. Rather, it was how the participants *interpreted* this cue, how they thought it *should* make them feel based on an array of previous experiences and social norms of the time in which they lived. Returning to the Internet as a tool, much of the coverage of Internet usage in the mass media paints a very negative picture of Internet use. Very rarely are positive outcomes of Internet use reported, for the sake of filling our heads with the dangers and nefarious intent of anyone and everyone who we might encounter online. The Internet itself does not create this negativity. It is how we use it, how we manage our self-presentations online, how we project ourselves to others, how we interpret others' behaviour towards us and how we invite that behaviour that may or may not make the Internet a dangerous place. The Internet itself is nothing other than a tool that human beings have adopted and adapted to meet their interaction and self-presentation requirements. It does not make people do things in any given manner. It does not make people misrepresent themselves or create an alter ego or persona with nefarious intent. People choose their actions and behaviour. They might be complying with external cues by responding in what they perceive to be a desired or wanted manner, but ultimately, they choose their own actions, either on the Internet or in the offline world. However, not all behaviours are guided by external cues or environmental stimuli. Internal cues also play a role, especially our interpretation of feelings, emotions or physiological arousal experienced in response to a given online stimulus. For example, a person's choice of behaviour might be influenced by a stagnated rage that hinders his/her ability to see beyond a currently felt emotion of anger or frustration, or of an overwhelming sexual draw to another individual, but ultimately the behavioural outcome is a choice made by the individual, even if this choice may sometimes be of an unconscious manner. The Internet in and of itself is therefore just another tool used in a chosen behaviour or behavioural response. It may enable people to do things that, for whatever reason, they feel unable to do offline. For instance, the Internet enables connections to hundreds, or even thousands, of people world-wide with similar interests, but it does not *make* those people connect.

DOI: 10.1057/9781137483416.0003

Unfortunately, there is a lot of negative media around individual self-portrayal across diverse Internet arenas. For the purposes of this text, the stance will be taken that it is more conducive to see the Internet as a tool that aids the execution of a wide and varied array of human behaviours. The motivations, drives and desires that underlie these choices will also be considered throughout this text.

1.7   Text overview

The next chapter of this book outlines a number of theoretical conceptualisations. Rather than repeatedly reporting these across the text, the reader can thus readily refer back to any given theory. Chapter 3 provides a more in-depth consideration of the role that individual factors play in online self-presentation, before looking at the ways in which people share information about the self online in Chapter 4. This chapter also explores the importance of the role of self-disclosure in conveying the motivations and desires of online self-representations before Chapter 5 considering in greater detail a number of social and social cognitive factors that impinge upon online impression management.

DOI: 10.1057/9781137483416.0003

2
Theoretical Considerations

Abstract: *Chapter 2 provides an overview of some of the most used theories to understand how people create, manipulate and maintain their online selves. Borrowing from various areas of offline psychology, online selves are considered according to classic theories of offline selves prior to outlining more up-to-date conceptualisations of understanding the online self. An overall case is built towards understanding online selves from a motivated and goal-directed approach.*

Key words: hyperpersonal communication; regulatory focus theory; self-discrepancy theory; uses and gratification; warranting

Attrill, Alison. *The Manipulation of Online Self-Presentation: Create, Edit, Re-edit and Present.* Basingstoke: Palgrave Macmillan, 2015. DOI: 10.1057/9781137483416.0004.

Living in a world surrounded by mass media that incessantly bombards us with an array of images, many of which promote certain lifestyles, body types and conveying an ideal life or body to be aspired to, it is no wonder that as societies, individuals from western cultures are becoming increasingly concerned with how they present themselves when partaking in this mass media. Human beings are not sponges; they do not simply soak up the material presented to them online. At a bare minimum there is some level of interpretation of content to which they are exposed, and to which they respond or ignore. The Internet is a two-way road; it can only thrive and exist through the content which people create and provide when using it. Think about websites such as *YouTube* which can only exist if people continue to post and share material. If no one uploads content, then there would be nothing to watch, nothing for a viewer to perceive, interpret or respond to. Thus, when representing the self online, people are not only consumers of the myriad of material which they may selectively choose to view or which they stumble upon per chance. They also actively take part in creating and propagating online material, including any ideals of self to which they and others may be exposed. The role of this constant influx of information into busy and hectic lives, and the way in which it shapes and influences the self, is wide and varied. It may cause people to question their own *body image*, their subjective perceptions about the self and how they think they look (e.g., Alipoor, Goodarzi, Nezhad & Zaheri, 2009), as well as playing around with peoples' notions of who they are (*actual self*), who they would like to be (*ideal self*) and who they think they should be (*ought self*). Turkle (1995) once noted that the Internet is a playground in which people can experiment with their different selves, where they can be who they want to be, who they may not be able to be offline, often under the guise of anonymity and the loss of a fear of social rejection (Pennebaker, 1989). Exploring this and associated notions, this chapter focuses on theoretical conceptualisations of how we create and edit our self-representations online. It outlines a number of the most often cited theories that have been applied to understanding how and why people create the selves that they create both offline and online along with how these might be subject to manipulation. It is important to note from the outset that each of the outlined theories deserves a chapter in its own right, but given the aim and brevity of this text, this chapter covers the most relevant points from each theory. To understand the cyberself, it is inevitable that some comparisons to offline selves will emerge throughout this and other chapters.

DOI: 10.1057/9781137483416.0004

2.1   Goffman's Theory of Self-Presentation

According to Goffman's Theory of Self-Presentation, the world is a stage upon which people perform their lives. Humans are but mere actors creating, interacting and responding to the world around them. Goffman further purported that most people strive to present themselves in a positive manner and in order to do so engage in what has become known as *impression management* (Chester & Bretherton, 2007). People use visual and verbal stimuli to present themselves offline. On considering how they create themselves on various different types of website, such as social networking sites (SNSs) and dating websites, they do indeed use visual stimuli, but rather than using spoken verbal stimuli, they rely on written text. There will, for instance, often be some level of self-populated description of the self in a way that is aimed to attract attention. Said description may be accompanied by photos, but on other websites such as Instagram or Pinterest, it is the photos that do the talking. On Pinterest, for example, people represent themselves through images that are not necessarily photos of themselves along with a limited number of characters. Posts often contain inspiring words or cryptic captions, leaving the viewer or reader with a guessing game as to the intentions of the poster. These methods of presenting the self are no different to those originally documented by Goffman's notion of humans being actors on the stage of life (see Section 1.5). The stage in this instance is merely whichever website one is presenting the self upon. The staging may differ, as may the way in which the act is carried out, but the intention of presenting oneself remains the same. That is not to say that this intention is always pre-meditated, or indeed even consciously considered, but rarely do people present self-information without some goal in mind (1959).

Before the adoption of the Internet for use by the masses in western cultures, Arkin (1981) proposed that there are two modes, or strategies, of self-presentation that can be used to manipulate and carry out the performance of life proposed by Goffman:

Acquisitive self-presentation: Used to *gain approval* from others through
    positive presentation of the self.
Protective self-presentation: Used to *avoid disapproval* from others through
    use of neutral and modest presentation of the self.

DOI: 10.1057/9781137483416.0004

Arkin (1981) goes on to propose that the human default is to use acquisitive self-presentation, switching to protective self-presentation under three conditions. First, if the presenting self (*presenter* or *poster*) is faced with unclear expectations from a target towards whom their self-presentation is directed (*recipient* or *target*), then the presenter will switch to avoid negative outcomes. Second, protective self-presentation is required to protect a presenter from undermining or negative disclosures or posts by the target. Finally, people may be naturally inclined to engage in protective rather than acquisitive self-presentation. Though acquisitive and protective self-presentations are both driven internally, by the individual's thoughts and interpretations and how they want others to perceive them, they could also serve to protect the individual from potential harm when presenting the cyberself. Both Arkin's and Goffman's theories emerged a considerable time before the modern Internet, making it difficult for the combination of the two theories to account for the array of other factors (e.g., technological, social or individual factors) that may come into play when portraying the self online (Rui & Stefanone, 2013). Consider again, the description in Chapter 1 (Section 1.4) of the diverse and ever-changing landscape of the Internet. Surely, any presenter not only needs to adapt their self-presentation to suit the particular Internet arena that they are using, but they also need to consider whom they are presenting the information to, and how that information is being presented. It could, for instance, be the case that when using a SNS, the intention is to gain approval from one's friends or acquaintances for a certain post shared. In this instance, it appears almost obvious that one would engage in acquisitive self-presentation tactics. If, however, a person was seeking information having been diagnosed with a sexually transmitted disease, s/he might want to seek advice from an online support or discussion group. The aim here would unlikely be to seek approval, but to avoid disapproval by using protective self-presentation. Indeed, in this instance it is likely that the presenter will use tactics such as creating a false identity or attempt to hide behind a screen name that has nothing to do with their real identity. That is, they may actively present a completely different self as part of their protective self-presentation.

Two important points emerge from this consideration of the theory of self-presentation and Arkin's notion of acquisitive and protective self-presentations. First, people appear able to adapt the types of

DOI: 10.1057/9781137483416.0004

self-presentation that they use depending upon the goals of that presentation and the type of Internet arena that they are using. Second, given that people may engage in manipulative self-presentations to protect themselves from disapproval, they could be selectively representing a completely different version of themselves online to offline. The next two theories to be considered outline how we might account for the presentation of these different selves.

2.2   Self-Discrepancy Theory, Regulatory Focus Theory and Flow Theory

One way to understand how people construct the self online is to borrow from theories of offline self-image and self-presentation management. One of the now classic theories of self is Higgins' Self-Discrepancy Theory (SDT) (1987). Higgins suggested that humans have three different representations of self: *actual, ideal* and *ought* selves. The *actual self* reflects who someone believes they actually are, their core self. It is their basic notion of who they really are, and how they think others believe them to consistently be. It is the bit of self that remains the same regardless of where they are, who they are with and what they are doing. An *ideal self* is the person who someone would really like to be, or aspires to be. One's notion of ideal self is what pushes them to do well, to have hopes, dreams and aspirations. It might be based on a role model or inspirational person from their social world, or be based on a famous or historical role model. The ideal self could thus be a self-constructed notion of one's self, or it could be based on comparisons to other people. Finally, the *ought self* is the person who somebody thinks they should be based on others' views and opinions, or based on societal norms to which they believe they should adhere. Although this is therefore the self that is regulated by expectations and demands from others, it is very much the individual's perception and interpretation of those expectations, views and social norms, among other factors, that leads to the construction and presentation of an ought self. Higgins laid the groundwork for many subsequent theories of self with this conceptualisation of different selves. A number of subsequent theories use the notion of different selves, with the most noticeable difference between them and SDT being that the actual self is called the *real, true* or *core* self. For example, Bargh, McKenna and Fitzsimons (2002) define a *true self* rather than an

DOI: 10.1057/9781137483416.0004

actual self as "those identity-important and phenomenally real aspects of self not often or easily expressed to others" (p. 34). Further theories of the self include Carver and Scheier's (1981, 1998) Control Theory of Self-Regulation, which sees people as persistently judging their self-concept against internal standards. Festinger's (1954) Social Comparison Theory suggests that people compare the self to others in such a way as to create a sense of individual identity and group belongingness, and Tesser's (1988) Self-Evaluation Maintenance Model suggests that people engage in either upward or downward comparisons to others in order to increase or reduce their positive sense of self. Most of these, and a multitude of other theories of self-construction and maintenance, are prevalent throughout a number of considerations as to how people create and present themselves online. If the reader is interested in these theories, then they can usually be found in greater detail in any basic introduction text to Social Psychology. Their inclusion here is merely for the illustration of awareness that Higgins' (1987) notion of actual, ideal and ought selves is not the only conceptualisation of self available. For the purposes of this text, the terms real, actual, core and true self will be used interchangeably as indicating that aspect of self that is tempo-rally and situationally consistent. The use of these terms in this way is substantiated through the finding that has often been interpreted as the actual self providing the core stability of self that gives meaning and consistency to one's life (e.g., Kernis & Goldman, 2006; Schlegel, Hicks, Arndt & King, 2009).

Schlegel, Vess and Arndt (2013) offer an overview of work carried out in this area, pointing out that having a positive understanding of one's actual self helps maintain a positive psychological sense of self (e.g., Bettencourt & Sheldon, 2001; Lakey, Kernis, Heppner & Lance, 2008; Ryan, LaGuardia & Rawsthorne, 2005; Sheldon, Ryan, Rawsthorne & Ilardi, 1997; Wood, Linely, Maltby, Baliousis & Joseph, 2008). Initial tests of online applications of theories of diverse selves to understanding presentation of the cyberself include Lee's (2004) consideration of how people use graphic representations of themselves in online gaming. Lee (2004) found that people mainly engaged in two types of online self-presentation. Whereas their use of a *para-authentic self* was considered to reflect the real or actual self online, creation of an *alter-self* was proposed to reflect the presentation of a completely different and unrepresenta-tive version of the real self. Lee uses the example of someone selecting a pictorial representation that is very different to the real self to create an

DOI: 10.1057/9781137483416.0004

alter-self online, suggesting that people can, and do, sometimes selectively choose between different versions of self to present online. What needs to be established, however, is why people choose the selected self to present online.

According to the basic SDT, one's psychological well-being is influenced by how well the match is between the three (actual, ideal and ought) selves. Imagine, for example, if while reading this you are dreaming of becoming the next winner of Britain's Got Talent, or the X-Factor, or any other talent show. That role of winner may become your ideal for which you are striving, but in reality you may be a student reading this text because you need the content for an exam. The latter reflects your real self. In this instance, a fair dose of reality might suggest that winning the X-Factor is an extremely unlikely prospect (unless of course you are a great singer), so the cleft between your ideal and actual selves is unlikely large enough or real enough to cause you psychological distress. If, however, your ideal self is to advance your actual student self to continue your studies to the ideal of achieving a PhD, then your actual self needs to be on track to achieve this goal. If your grades were to slip drastically below a required entry grade for PhD level study, then you might become distressed at the prospect of not achieving your ideal self status. There are ample literary examples of differences between ideal and actual selves, especially in relation to body image, weight, size and social status, with the *perceived* gap between the two selves being of importance for levels of psychological well-being. This perceived gap is based on how all three selves are evaluated against an individual's own values and norms, which Higgins called *self-guides*. In particular, the actual self acts as an internal self-guide against which thoughts and actions can be evaluated in terms of their meaning and value (e.g., Schlegel & Hicks, 2011; Schlegel et al., 2009). When consciously considering a route of action, a person may choose how to present themselves based on previous similar presentations and outcomes thereof. They might think about the way in which the presentation is in line with their self-guides. On doing so, they may assess whether there is a discrepancy between these self-guides and the intended actual or ideal self-presentation. In order to reduce the discrepancy, they may then choose a more actual self-presentation. In line with this proposal, some reports suggest that when a person is faced with somewhat difficult behavioural decisions, they are most likely to use a presentation of the true self to arrive at a decision which they feel they can subsequently justify (e.g., Baumeister, 1999; Bellah, Madsen,

DOI: 10.1057/9781137483416.0004

Sullivan, Swidler & Tipton, 1985). To elaborate, if you have to make a difficult choice between saying or doing something upon which you might subsequently be judged, it is more likely that you will make a decision that is in line with who you perceive yourself to actually be. You will be more able to subsequently justify the decision you made, both to yourself and whoever may be affected by that decision. Knowing your actual self is thus very important to the perception, interpretation and responses to your own and others' thoughts, feelings and behaviours. Nonetheless, people do sometimes present an ideal or ought self, and the Internet offers them a rather large playground for doing so. The notion of ideal self-presentation online has gathered momentum again in recent years, having been one of the first concepts put forward by Turkle (1995) in relation to online self-presentation. In particular, research is emerging that focuses on how people use the Internet to explore an ideal self which can then be transferred offline as their actual self.

An example of how people use the Internet to explore and find acceptance for their actual self is provided by DeHaan, Kuper, Magee, Bigelow and Mustanski (2013). These researchers offer an excellent consideration of how lesbian, gay, bisexual and transgender (LGBT) youths use Internet support systems and resources to face and overcome obstacles that they feel are unique to them offline. In a study that found the Internet to provide information and support to LGBT youths in such a way as to enhance their offline quality of life, DeHaan et al. (2013) carried out semi-structured interviews with 32 LGBT individuals. They found that the youths may hide core aspects of their actual self in order to avoid the judgements they may face in their offline worlds (Mustanski, Newcomb & Garofalo, 2011), whereas the Internet offers them an opportunity to explore and express aspects of this self, possibly in a way that enhances their levels of feeling accepted. The more they do this, the more they might engage in Arkin's (1981) acquisitive self-presentation techniques. DeHaan et al. (2013) outline studies that have demonstrated the use of the Internet to increase a feeling of closeness in a way that can help LGBT youths find self-acceptance and enhance their offline quality of life (e.g., Bargh, McKenna & Fitzsimons, 2002; Hillier & Harrison, 2007). They also provide evidence for the aforementioned two way flow of the Internet in that the youths' needs and desires may be met by using the Internet, but it is their offline lives that guided and influenced the online behaviours carried out to meet those needs. In other words, while the youths were seeking out material to foster their positive self-image, it

DOI: 10.1057/9781137483416.0004

was likely the actual or core self which would have prompted them to do so in the first place. This raises the question as to what would happen if a person did not receive the sought affirmation of their actual self when presented online. This brings us to the discrepancies that could arise in how people reconcile their actual, ideal and ought selves.

2.2.1 Self-discrepancies

A discrepancy between any two of the actual, ideal and ought selves can potentially cause psychological discomfort or damage to an individual. Higgins (1987) suggests that different discrepancies underlie different psychological vulnerabilities. In particular, two regulatory systems are involved in maintaining the self, an *ideal self-regulatory system* that is based on the presence or absence of positive outcomes, and an *ought self-regulatory system* based on the presence or absence of negative outcomes. When positive outcomes are absent, dejection-related emotions are experienced, and when negative outcomes are absent, emotions commonly associated with agitation are experienced. These are further conceptualised by Higgins (1997) in his Regulatory Focus Theory (RFT) as *promotion* and *prevention,* both of which revolve around the notion of goal-directed behaviour that either promotes a positive outcome or prevents a negative outcome. These can be likened to Arkin's (1981) notion of acquisitive and protective strategies: *Promotion strategies* are akin to Arkin's acquisitive strategies and are based on hopes and/or aspirations employed specifically to evoke a positive outcome. Typical promotion strategies include people seeking specific accomplishments and advancement through targeted (or goal-directed) actions. *Prevention strategies,* which are similar to Arkin's protective strategies, result from a sense of duty or obligation and are employed to avoid negative outcomes. These can occur, for example, when people employ goal-directed tactics to seek out safety and security. Employing either of these strategies could thus enhance or reduce a discrepancy in either of the self-regulatory systems. To illustrate RFT and the associated strategies, consideration is given to how SDT has been applied to online behaviours.

There are a few research examples available that consider the use of SDT to explore how individuals internalise unrealistic images that they often experience in the mass media (e.g., Myers & Biocca, 1992; Tiggemann & Mcgill, 2004; Tiggemann & Slater, 2004). To maintain a good and healthy self-image, people need to have confidence in their own body image and in their actual selves. In pre-Internet times, they

DOI: 10.1057/9781137483416.0004

might have been exposed to image ideals and notions of the perfect self, but these may not have been as intrusive and damaging as those images that now enter homes on a more frequent basis. Consider for example, the perfect body size for a woman. This has consistently changed over time, with Marilyn Monroe being the voluptuous ideal in the 1950s and a supermodel size zero becoming an ideal in the 1990s. These ideals were portrayed in magazines, posters adverts and television commercials. They were based on celebrities who individuals aspired to imitate, but they were not persistently shown on the array of intrusive mass media now experienced. Nowadays, unrealistic ideals are not only perpetuated by the mass media, but are also learned through social media. It is not unheard of that regular people who use SNSs use photo editing tools prior to uploading images to their social media pages to create a more perfect image of self for presentation. Consider for a moment some of the pictures that you might see of your friends on Facebook and ask yourself whether these are representations of the posters' true self. While there are good reasons as to why people may want to present themselves in the best possible manner, people are now exposed from a young age to pictorial ideals of people who they may perceive to be attainable role models, rather than the unattainable ideals of half a century ago. These ideals could become internalised as their own standards and self-guides to which they later compare their actual selves. These edited ideals of people we actually know and interact with thus shape ideal selves via interactions online in a way that the mass media could hitherto not achieve. Use of social media may actually enhance the cleft between ideal and ought selves in such a way as to evoke more self-discrepancies, especially those belonging to the ideal self-regulatory system than thus far considered in the offline world.

Work is emerging that has considered SDT and RFT in online spheres to test self-discrepancies and their effects on individuals' sense of self. Kim and Sundar (2012), for example, assigned participants to one of four avatar conditions for an interaction in the virtual environment of Second Life (www.secondlife.com) (*customise ideal self avatar; customise actual self avatar; assigned attractive avatar; assigned unattractive avatar*). The use of different avatars evoked different mental images in participants of their own physical appearance in this study, which then influenced whether they engaged in prevention or promotion strategies in their interactions. Of particular interest is the observation that participants who used an avatar based on their ideal self body image were more motivated to

DOI: 10.1057/9781137483416.0004

engage in preventative behaviours in Second Life. This makes sense. If you created an ideal version of your self and put that onto a virtual environment such as Second Life, then you would be rather hurt or upset if someone criticised that ideal self. Therefore, in order to avoid that happening, you may engage in preventative strategies so that you can keep up the appearance of an ideal, at least for the time in which you are engaged in the virtual environment. This raises an interesting question for future research, namely whether people can use the Internet in such a manner as to create ideals online that they can then transfer offline, but without the preventative strategy engagement. To fulfil the latter criteria, the online actors would need to be able to accept their online selves as their actual offline selves and subsequently engage in promotion rather than preventive strategies. Currently, theories of self would suggest that the types of acceptance and promotion engaged in may be embedded as part of one's self-concept.

An individual's *self-concept* is the individual's overall notion of the self (e.g., Markus & Nurius, 1986) which comprises many facets of self-knowledge, including the actual, ideal and ought selves, autobiographical knowledge and memories, information related to the self about other people, as well as psychological evaluations that result in levels of *self-esteem* (perceived positive or negative evaluation of the self) and *self-efficacy* (one's own perceived ability in a task). When a person is at one with their world, when there is no discrepancy between the different types of self, a person experiences what Campbell, Trapnell, Heine, Katz, Lavallee and Lehman (1996) refer to as *self-concept clarity*. It is beyond the scope of this book to consider how this self-concept clarity is achieved both offline and online. It is, however, worth noting that there remains an ongoing debate as to whether people develop or create their self-concept. Of particular importance for this text is that both creation and development could take place online. Let us consider both possibilities. If the self is *developed* from early childhood onwards, then it could be assumed that it becomes more or less fixed at some point in life. We know, however, that the existence of at least the three different selves (actual, ideal and ought) which are malleable and flexible suggests that even if this development takes place, the self can be edited and recreated at any point. That is not to say that a newly created self-concept is necessarily sustainable, but it can be suggested that this recreation may take place on the Internet. If the real or actual self is *created* rather than developed over a certain period of life, the outcome would be the same – the

DOI: 10.1057/9781137483416.0004

self can still be edited and recreated and subsequently presented to suit one's current notion of actual or ideal self. Although we might assume that the ability to create online any version of self that one wishes to may be more in line with the creationist view, Schlegel et al. (2013) point out that a creation of self implies no existence of an underlying self. If the underlying self is considered to be one's core self, then it would be virtually impossible to sustain any creation of self that was not based on the actual self, since there would unlikely be a core self that remained the same across time and situations. This we know not to be the case. In addition, such a construction would surely mean that the self would be in a constant state of change based on situational cues and factors, change that would evoke discrepancies in self-identity and instability to one's psychological well-being. If that was the case, people would never achieve an ongoing positive and satisfied sense of self, regardless of whether their self-presentation is taking place online or offline.

2.2.2 Flow Theory

One theory that could be used in conjunction with SDT and RFT relating to creating a positive sense of self, and that is experiencing a resurgence in considerations around presenting the self online is Csikszentmihalyi's (1975) flow theory. According to Csikszentmihalyi, a state of psychological flow is achieved when one experiences a complete loss of self-awareness due to an enjoyable experience. There is usefulness of considering flow theory in relation to video gaming. Many gamers use online or video gaming as an escapism, as the experience of gaming offers them the opportunity to be someone else, to flee their offline life and to immerse themselves in a world that enables them to play around with their self-concept. Prior to the Internet, they may have immersed themselves in offline activities that enabled them to flee aspects of their daily lives, such as watching television or reading a book. In doing so, they may have fantasised about an ideal self constructed through the pages of a favourite book, or they may have dreamt of a job or social role based on characters from films or television series. Indeed, Zillman (1982) notes the use of television as an escape from a life of drudgery. Using technology or media to create an alternative version of self is therefore not necessarily a new concept. Over the last decade, the notion of flow and how it might affect self concept has been explored in a number of studies, involving the demonstration that the four major factors of *playfulness, skill, telepresence* and *time distortion* play a role in

DOI: 10.1057/9781137483416.0004

deriving a positive sense of flow (Novak, Hoffman & Yung, 2000). Lee, Aiken and Hung (2012) also found that people who had a less clear notion of their offline self-concept were more likely to spend longer playing video games, and that an experience of flow was more positively related to the amount of time spent playing. This would suggest that people who have a less developed sense of self concept may use video games to create a version of the self that enables them to experience a state of psychological equilibrium not necessarily achieved offline. They may use gaming as a form of escapism without it necessarily impacting upon their own perceived offline self. In order to do so, they may create a persona online that is so distinct and diverse from their offline self that the player completely distinguishes between the two.

Thus far, the self has been considered as being presented in one of its three main guises with no cross-over in that presentation. It has very much been presented as a goal-directed either/or scenario. This may not necessarily be the case. The self may be far more fluid or far more distinct than has been considered. While the jury appears to remain out on this particular argument, for the remainder of this text, I will align with those who perceive the self and one's identity to be a fluid and malleable construct that shifts in time, situations and the people encountered (see e.g., McCarthey & Moje, 2002).

2.3   Social Information Processing Theory and the Hyperpersonal Communication Model

One feature of online communication that is not considered by SDT, RFT or flow theory is the methods used to create a version of self online and how these differ greatly from offline modes of communication and interactions. The first communication tools available to the general public via the Internet were based on different forms of text communication such as emails and chat room exchanges. Much early research around online self-presentation and communication focused on how people needed to construct the self in written format online, often focusing on there being no *social cues* available. Social cues are any external indicators of behaviour. They can be features associated with people such as body language, facial expression and voice intonation, or aspects of the environment, such as being in a hostile or friendly situation. Humans tend to use these cues in order to interpret and respond to a situation or person(s). If on

DOI: 10.1057/9781137483416.0004

a date, for example, your date leans towards you and smiles, you would likely interpret this body language as the person showing an interest in you. It is exactly this sort of non-verbal communication that was initially considered absent online. However, humans are nothing if not adaptive. For centuries the human race has evolved and not only adapted to their environment, but also exploited the environment and all of its tools to work for them. It is no wonder then that humans soon found ways to compensate online for the absence of social cues found in offline communication and interactions.

This compensation and adaptation is the focus of Walther's (1992) Social Information Processing Theory (SIP). One of the basic premises of SIP is that people can adapt to compensate for any missing cues in online text-based communications. Considering that most early communications and interactions on the Internet occurred via written text, it is conceivable that what is read online, how it is interpreted and reactions to it help shape one's understanding of both one's self and other people as well as evoking images of how these people may look and/or act. The written word is very powerful when creating an understanding of one's own and others' identities. People also derive images and understanding of others from how they construct themselves in written communications, how they describe themselves and how they frame themselves within a given context using written text. This notion was also noted by McCarthey and Moje (2002) who drew on Vygotsky's (1978) proposals that from a very young age people internalise knowledge and beliefs from the world around them. McCarthey and Moje (2002) point out that what people read along with other forms of media that they absorb and process, influences how they make sense of the world, which in turn affects how they perceive themselves as existing within that world. In online communication nowadays, if constructing the self in written text, people often use symbols or emoticons (e.g., ☺ ☹) to convey non-visible emotions and feelings. They might also use a hashtag (#) in an attempt to create popularity of a statement or topic which they are discussing or promoting. It is also becoming more commonplace to attach photographs of locations from which one is messaging or posting, or to include a picture of oneself with the people of a certain event. The rate at which humans have accepted modern technology into their everyday lives could be somewhat alarming when considering how they have very quickly developed such interactive communications tools. This adoption does not however always ensue

DOI: 10.1057/9781137483416.0004

for newer technologies across all forms of online communication. Rai and Attrill (2014) found recently, for instance, that people were very reluctant to use video communication, especially if communicating with someone outside of immediate family circles. Even if video communication gathers popularity in the future, it would nonetheless raise the question as to whether this can be conceived of as replicating the cues felt and experienced in offline communications. Given that the self that people bring to such an online exchange is not instantly constructed for that exchange, it may be likely that those people who would be more prepared to use video communication may be those who are more comfortable with presenting the actual self and who are less worried about impression management online. These speculations clearly offer an exciting avenue of research that requires the exploration of many more factors than the mere presence or absence of social cues in written communication. Although there is still some work to be carried out around this particular aspect of presenting the self online, Walther (1996) subsequently developed a theory to consider what happens when people start using the absence of social cues online to their advantage.

In the Hyperpersonal Communication Model (HCM), Walther (1996) proposed that computer-mediated communication (CMC) enables individuals to use the absence of cues to their advantage in both synchronous and asynchronous modes of communication. It should be noted that Walther (1996) has revised his theory a number of times to consider other factors that play a role in CMC. He suggests that sometimes online interactions become *hyperpersonal* to individuals, that is, they become more important and significant to them than their offline communications. The aspect of HCM that is of interest here, however, is how people use different types of CMC to create the cyberself. Whereas *synchronous communication* occurs in real time, with immediate responses (e.g., video chat or instant messenger), *asynchronous communication* has delayed responses in lapsed time (e.g., email or social networking site status updates). Walther proposed that individuals take advantage of asynchronous modes of communication in order to compensate for the absence of social cues. They can take their time to craft responses to present the self in a positive light. It could also be suggested that asynchronous communication promotes acquisitive self-presentation strategies (Ellison, Heino & Gibbs, 2006; see also Arkin, 1981). This does not imply, however, that synchronous communication elicits protective self-presentation. This will very much depend upon how much input there is from others to an

DOI: 10.1057/9781137483416.0004

individual's synchronous communication. Asynchronous communication allows users to create, edit and present more of an ideal self as it gives them time to think about and compose content relevant to their desired self-presentation. They can compensate for having no social cues by constructing text descriptions to evoke images and portrayals of a self who they wish to be. As a reader, you might be wondering how this could work in email. After all, email is rarely consciously used to foster or promote a certain self image, or is it? Every time you construct an email, you are in fact revealing something of yourself to the recipient(s). Even if that something is how formal or informal you are in your communications. Next time you construct or reply to an email, consider whether you ponder what you are writing or whether you simply frantically type, do not read what you have written and hit the send button. My guess is that you will likely change your email construction strategy depending upon who you are communicating with. If you want someone to see you in a positive light, then you will likely give your communication more thought and consideration while attempting to avoid any miscommunication of your email content.

Synchronous communication may not always be as in time as it might first appear. When using video-communications tools such as *Skype* or *FaceTime*, users have a number of social cues which make this type of communication more instant and reflective of face-to-face (FtF) interactions than say instant messaging. Instant messaging, while occurring in real time, still enables the user to create and carefully edit a response before sending it to a communications partner. When using SNSs, people might engage in what they believe to be an asynchronous communication such as a status update, but this may turn into a more or less synchronous exchange if other people instantly reply to the post. In this instance, regardless of how carefully a person has created and crafted their self-image to reflect their desired self, the input from others might (1) offer a more accurate reflection of the poster's true or real self, and (2) cause the poster to switch from acquisitive to protective self-presentation. This observation along with much of this discussion around Walther's HCM could be taken to suggest that people use CMC in a goal-directed way. If we take the email example above, there is an assumption that by carefully crafting the email, the sender is engaging in impression management tactics because they want to make a certain impression on the recipient(s). If this is the case, then a theory that considers this goal-directed component to presenting the self online may be able to shed

DOI: 10.1057/9781137483416.0004

some light onto why this type of impression management ensues even in what might be perceived to be non-considered communications.

2.4   Uses and Gratifications Theory

When considering the Internet to be a tool that is used in a goal-directed manner in conjunction with the notion that individuals strive to create both a positive image of self and a sense of flow by reducing discrepancies between their actual, ideal and ought selves, it is likely that people use the Internet in a motivated manner to fulfil psychological or behavioural goals. This proposal is in line with the basic premises of Uses and Gratifications Theory (U&G) (Katz, Blumler & Gurevitch, 1973). Goals come in many shapes and forms and differ from one person to the next. They can be behavioural, psychological, physical, cognitive or a mixture of any of these and many more facets of human nature. For example, one person's goal online might be to meet a new lifetime partner while another person's goal might be to use the Internet to obtain new employment. Both goals require a self-representation that may be tailored and managed to achieve the desired outcome of a date or employment. The self-presentation in each situation would likely vary. In terms of U&G theory, the Internet is used to gratify the desired outcome or need.

There are some theorists who suggest that many behavioural goals are driven by underlying human needs, from the desire for a sense of human belonging (e.g., Deci & Ryan, 2000; Baumeister & Leary, 1995), to the fulfilment of social needs otherwise not met in the offline world (Davis & Kraus, 1989). On considering the basic human need to feel wanted, liked and connected to both smaller groups, such as intimate relationships, and larger social groups such as families and cultural groups (e.g., Deci & Ryan, 2000), U&G theory could be used to suggest that the gratification of achieving this overall sense of belonging may be created by using the Internet. Taking this a step further, if this gratification is not achieved offline, a person may create a version of self online to evoke and promote fulfilment of the need. They might engage in *social compensation* for this aspect of everyday life that may be absent offline. In line with this notion, McKenna, Green and Gleason (2002) suggested that people may use the Internet to achieve social compensation if they feel inhibited in their social interactions offline. Valkenburg, Schouten and Peter (2005) proposed, on the other hand, that the online self is an

DOI: 10.1057/9781137483416.0004

extension of one's offline self with individuals behaving similarly both offline and online. Evidence to support Valkenburg et al.'s *social enhancement* proposal comes from Papacharissi and Mendelson (2011) who observed that individuals socially active offline benefited more from their online social networking behaviours than did those less socially active offline. Whether using the Internet to present a distinct self or an extended self, U&G theory demonstrates that it is possibly be used as a tool to fulfil basic human needs and desires, a concept returned to in numerous sections throughout the remainder of this book.

Although some of the conceptualisations outlined thus far consider self-presentation and impression management online, the online poster rarely operates as a secluded, non-involved entity. Rather they are exposed to information about other people, events and objects. This information can influence their self-perceptions and how they relate to others, as can posts about them by others. Attention therefore now turns to the final theory in this chapter to consider how information from other online sources is processed and integrated into one's own self-image and self-presentation processes.

2.5 Warranting Theory

As outlined throughout this book thus far, when sharing information about oneself online, people are able to carefully construct and edit that information to manage others' impressions of them. Though it is often overlooked that other people also do this, some work suggests that people are sometimes sceptical about information posted by others online because they are aware of the impression management processes involved in such presentations (e.g., Caspi & Gorsky, 2006). With this knowledge in mind, Walther and Parks (2002) proposed that posters will often use their own self-guides and values to evaluate whether others' offline self-information matches their online selves, an evaluation process that was subsequently called a *warranting value* by Walther (2011). *Warranting* is the term now given to a cue that can be used to verify someone's online self as an accurate extension or representation of their offline self. DeAndrea (2014) explains a warranting value as a psychological construct that is used to consider whether information posted online about a person can be manipulated by the person it describes. A warranting value is thus used to lend credence to information that might be used to form an impression of others in a cost-benefit type evaluation that occurs when someone is judging online information as an accurate representation of another person. This evaluation has become known as the *warranting principle* and suggests that the less controlled posts about others are perceived to be by the subject of those posts, the more they will be considered to be accurate representations of the real or actual self of the topic matter (Walther, Van Der Heide, Hamel & Schulman, 2009). In colloquial terms, you might be familiar with the saying "it came straight from the horse's mouth" to imply credibility to the source of information to which you are referring. The warranting principle acts in much the same way. Imagine that you have met someone on a dating website and you want to ascertain the level of their actual self-presentation. You might ask to be added to their social networking site profile to consider what other people say about that person on their wall. If what you read matches the description of the person you have met, on the dating website you might assume high credibility of their self-presentations. If, however, the person has portrayed themselves in a completely different manner to the way other people describe them, you might question the value of their own self-portrayal. Warranting is thus very helpful and informative in judging whether another person is providing a representation of their actual self online. Evidence to this effect comes from DeAndrea's (2014) report on a number of studies that have shown third-party comments to affect perceivers' impressions of the comment subject, including work by Antheunis and Schouten (2011) which found that perceived levels of social attractiveness were affected by third-party comments. DeAndrea (2014) also points out that third-party comments can often be edited or controlled by the person to whom the content relates. However, posters put themselves at risk of a reduced warranting value should they manage impressions of themselves via third-party comments. The value is also reduced through high levels of perceived control and impression management through restrictions of who can access third-party claims or comments. These considerations raise a number of questions for future research, including the question as to whether it is more difficult to create and maintain false or inaccurate representations of self in exactly those online arenas where one might want to manipulate and manage presentation of their self to the fullest benefits.

One of the recurring themes throughout this text is the notion of people being able to edit and manipulate their online self-presentations. Taken together, the theories outlined in this chapter would suggest that people

DOI: 10.1057/9781137483416.0004

are very much able to flexibly present and manipulate their online selves, but there are a number of factors that have not been incorporated into these theories, to which attention will turn in the next three chapters of this text, individual factors (Chapter 3), motivations and self-disclosure (Chapter 4) and social and social cognitive factors (Chapter 5).

DOI: 10.1057/9781137483416.0004

3

Individual Factors and the Cyberself

Abstract: *The interaction of personality and individual characteristics with online behaviour is a convoluted relationship. This chapter attempts to pick apart some of the links between various personality factors such as loneliness, shyness and depression, and different online activities. It also provides a focus on social networking behaviour from a motivated understanding of human beings needing to feel as if they are wanted, belong and are liked. Consideration is also given to the notion of the Internet providing all individuals the opportunity to engage in naïve psychological attempts at understanding peoples' online self-presentations.*

Key words: individual factors; naïve psychologies; personality characteristics; social networking sites

Attrill, Alison. *The Manipulation of Online Self-Presentation: Create, Edit, Re-edit and Present.* Basingstoke: Palgrave Macmillan, 2015. DOI: 10.1057/9781137483416.0005.

DOI: 10.1057/9781137483416.0005

One area of research that has received attention relating to the creation and maintenance of the self online is that of personality. *Personality* can be defined as those characteristics that come together to provide a person with consistency in his/her behaviours across times and situations, but which also create individual differences between people (e.g., Pervin, 1993). They are the traits that make people similar yet unique. As outlined in Chapter 2, a number of theories have suggested that individuals have a number of different selves. In particular, attention was paid to Higgins' (1987) Self-Discrepancy Theory which outlined the *actual self* (one's core and consistent self across time and situations), the *ideal self* (who one would really like to be) and the *ought self* (who one believes they should be based on social norms and others' views and opinions). A lot of work has considered how these selves are represented online, and whether cyberselves are more a reflection of true or ideal selves. Turkle (1997) is probably one of the most cited researchers in this area, given her early suggestions of the Internet as a laboratory in which people can explore facets of their different selves in a way that enables persistent creation and recreation of the self. One feature not considered by the theories outlined in Chapter 2, however, is the role that individual characteristics may play in (1) driving those representations and explorations and (2) the way in which those representations and explorations influence an individual's personality. This chapter focuses on research that has been carried out to consider exactly these roles as well as the interaction of personality and online self-presentation.

3.1   Personality characteristics and markers

In a paper that explores the way in which people express different aspects of their personalities across different contexts, Clifton (2014) employs a *social network analysis* (SNA) approach to understanding the cyberself. Offline, a social network comprises of the people with whom one interacts. Online, the term *social network* has become synonymous with interactive websites such as Facebook which enable people to create and maintain social links to a variety of different people, some of whom they might know offline, some of whom they may never meet offline but have met through a shared common interest or connection to another person online. These social networks are denoted through the use of the abbreviation SNS – social networking site (SNSs plural). One's social

DOI: 10.1057/9781137483416.0005

networks online (SNs) reflect the different online groups to which they belong. One of the first social networks established online was *The Big Sky Telegraph* (Odasz, 1991). This group consisted of more than 50 schools and libraries that were linked via the Internet as a low-cost educational sharing exercise to test the use of online networking as a societal tool. Though the network soon diminished and ran into technological and monetary difficulties, it offered an insight into one of the first online social networks which provided a model for any future SNs. It is this type of social network that is the focus of Clifton's (2014) SNA.

In Clifton's (2014) SNA, participants' relationships with 30 members of their chosen social network were quantified according to the *Big Five* personality factors (characteristics). These are the five characteristics most often used in research that considers any aspect of personality. McCrae and Costa (1987) *OCEAN Model* consists of *openness, conscientiousness, extraversion, agreeableness* and *neuroticism*. Each of these five factors is, in turn, summarised by various *personality markers*. For example, if a person is very anxious and moody (personality markers), the overarching category label given to these traits would be neurotic. Each of the dimensions included in the OCEAN Model exist along a continuum. Although being described as either extravert or introvert, for instance, it might be the case that a person falls more towards one end than the other of the continuum of extraversion. It should be noted that while focus is given here to the OCEAN model, there are a number of other trait models of personality that have been applied to understanding online self-presentation. If you want to find out more about these different models, then a good starting point can be found at this Internet address: http://www.personalityresearch.org/bigfive.html. For the sake of brevity and clarity, focus is given here to the basic OCEAN model. A brief overview of the five overarching categories of traits and some of their associated markers now follows:

Openness: People who score high on openness are open to new experiences. They are often characterised as having unusual thought processes and thinking outside the box, while remaining curious and introspective. Open individuals have been shown to be more likely to post personal information on SNSs than less open people (Amichai-Hamburger & Vinitzky, 2010).

Conscientiousness: High conscientiousness scorers value detail, are often described as efficient and organised, as well as being

DOI: 10.1057/9781137483416.0005

considered reliable. They are often self-disciplined while maintaining a sense of dutifulness and striving for achievement. Conscientious individuals have been shown to be more cautious online and to present themselves in a more agreeable and compliant manner to the medium in which they are presenting themselves. They have also been shown to be more consistent in their online self-presentations, which are often in line with their actual self (e.g., Leary & Allen, 2011).

Extraversion: Extravert individuals are often described as outgoing, energetic and enthusiastic. They are generally considered to be gregarious while their counterpart *introverts* are quiet and reserved. People who are often assertive, talkative and seek excitement are thought of as extravert. Probably one of the most researched of the five OCEAN traits, a lot of work has assessed extravert and introverts' online activities. There are however conflicting demonstrations, with Bibby (2008) showing higher levels of sharing self-relevant information by extraverts while Amichai-Hamburger and Vinitzky (2010) observed the opposite: Extraverts shared less personal information on SNSs. There may be a number of reasons for this discrepancy, including that the two studies may have differentially assessed levels of sharing. This discrepancy will be further explored later in this chapter.

Agreeableness: If a person is appreciative, compliant, modest and trusting, they are often described as agreeable. Agreeable individuals do not like to rock the boat. They like to appear consistent and non-critical. Leary and Allen (2011) found that agreeable individuals were more likely to present their actual self on SNSs.

Neuroticism: If a person displays high levels of anxiety, persistent worrying and is often self-conscious to the point of appearing hostile, s/he might be described as being highly neurotic. Neurotic individuals are also considered to be impulsive, self-defeating and often unstable in their self-presentations and actions. There is some evidence to suggest that neurotic individuals may seek a connection with others via the Internet that they may not experience in their offline world (e.g., Forest and Wood, 2012).

This brief overview of the OCEAN model would suggest that personalities are a fixed entity. They are not. From the outline of the self-discrepancy model in Chapter 2, it could be assumed that these characteristics

DOI: 10.1057/9781137483416.0005

and traits help construct one's core personality. In line with this proposal, some theories of personality suggest that people have core and peripheral personality traits that become more or less salient based on situational and external factors (e.g., Eysenck & Eysenck, 1985). Although one's core personality might thus provide the consistency with which one presents the self, some characteristics and traits may guide people to behave differently and present different versions of self depending upon the activity or situation in which they are engaged. For the purposes of this text, it is assumed that one's core personality is that aspect of the self that remains consistent in reflecting one's actual or true self.

As previously mentioned, all five of the OCEAN traits exist on a continuum, with everyone falling at some point along each of those continua. The model thus lends itself to considering many facets of online self-representations. Examples of such research include that which has attempted to establish the extent to which each of these characteristics can be used to understand whether online representations are in line with peoples' perceptions of their actual self. A couple of meta-analytic reviews have established that expressions of extraversion, openness and conscientiousness appear to be most consistent with perceptions of one's real self, with the role of agreeableness and neuroticism in self-presentation presenting a less clear picture (e.g., Connelly & Ones, 2010; Connolly, Kavanagh & Viswesvaran, 2007). Understanding the role of neuroticism appears to pose the biggest challenge to researchers given that it appears to be the most difficult of the five personality markers to identify both in the self and others, online and offline (e.g., Gill, Oberlander & Austin, 2006; Marcus, Machilek & Schutz, 2006; Back, Stopfer, Vazire, Gaddiss, Schmuckle, Egloff & Gosling, 2010). Consider how difficult you might find it to detect the different personality markers in people with whom you interact online, especially if you are attempting to detect these from written text. If you were to ask five close friends with whom you interact online and five acquaintances who you do not know so well to give you written descriptions of themselves, would you be able to detect their core personality from these descriptions? What about if you asked them to accompany that description with a photograph? Would that aid the quest to identify their traits? As outlined in Walther's (1996) Hyperpersonal Communications Theory in Chapter 2, social cues play a role in understanding portrayals of both the self and others. Therefore, if you compared your original ten descriptions to another ten which were presented to you via video communication, you

DOI: 10.1057/9781137483416.0005

might think that identifying and interpreting the traits would be easier given that video reinstates some of the social cues that might help this recognition. The point here is to illustrate that different modes of communication might make recognition of core personality traits more or less easy online. Unfortunately, there are inconsistencies in findings that have been reported relating to these considerations with inconsistencies being shown in the ability to recognise some traits using web-chats (Rouse & Haas, 2003) and video-conferencing (Okdie, Guadagno, Bernieri, Geers & Mclarney-Vesotski, 2011). Marriott and Buchanan (2014) provide a good overview of a number of findings relating to the suggestion that a lot of the studies which have considered recognising portrayals of characteristics in line with one's own and others' true selves often had participants rate complete strangers. They argue that people are more likely to express their true self, and recognise that they are doing so, in prolonged online interactions. Over time, communicators will likely build up a rapport and get to know one another, which should make identifying one another's true selves and associated characteristics easier.

In a study in which they gauged whether people are more likely to express their true self online or offline, Marriott and Buchanan (2014) had 523 participants and 258 observers complete *personality*, *Real Me* and *shyness* measures. The observers were people nominated by and known to the participants. They found no evidence of participants being more or less likely to present a real self online than offline, with no influence of personality traits in predicting who would present their actual self online. One of the reasons that the authors offer for interpreting the absence of difference in presenting the self online and offline is that people are becoming so used to having the Internet in their daily lives that it has simply become an extension of their offline world (see also Correa, Hinsley & Gil de Zuniga, 2010). This line of reasoning would suggest that it is no longer the case that people use the Internet to explore their hidden identities as once proposed by Turkle (1995), but that they use it as an extension of their offline selves. Marriott and Buchanan (2014) cite research from Gosling, Augustine, Vazire, Holtzman and Gaddis (2011) to support this proposal, in which SNSs were considered as an extension of one's offline social world, rather than as stand-alone tools for self-exploration.

Thus far, consideration has been given to whether people recognise their own and others' personality traits from online portrayals using

DOI: 10.1057/9781137483416.0005

different modes of communication and whether personality traits play a role in people being more or less likely to present an accurate presentation online rather than offline. Another of the difficulties in establishing the interplay between personality traits and online self-presentation besides these considerations is that people may allow different aspects of the personality to influence how they portray themselves across different types of Internet website. Given the explosion in use of SNSs over the past few years, it is not surprising that a lot of work has focused on how people present themselves on these types of website. Focus will therefore now be given to exploring further some of the work that has considered SNSs.

3.2   Social networking sites

Quite a lot of work around personality and Internet use has focused on SNSs, in particular on Facebook. This is most likely due to the majority of work being carried out in western cultures in which Facebook has become the most popular SNS. It is worth noting that other countries and cultures have different SNSs that have overtaken Facebook use. China's QZone, for example, had 625 million monthly active users in February 2014 (www.statista.com). Most SNSs have certain features in common that necessitate some level of self-presentation. They require individuals to create a written profile which displays their basic demographic information such as location, schools attended, current employment, relationship status and details about one's family members. They also usually offer the opportunity to engage with people who one has added as friends via different modes of communication, including the most private form which is instant messaging or mailing, and the less private wall posts. Depending upon the settings chosen by the user, a limited set of people may be able to see and/or respond to anything posted on their wall. These are usually the people who one has added as friends. There are often a number of other display and response options, including that everything can be viewed but not responded to by the general public, and that no one, not even friends can post or respond to anything on one's wall. It is somewhat forgivable that research in this area has focused largely on Facebook given that most individuals see this as first of these SNSs that was available to the mass population. The reader is directed to Boyd and Ellison's (2007) work on SNSs for a fuller overview

DOI: 10.1057/9781137483416.0005

of perceptions of different SNS as well as to a very recent article from the British Psychological Society (http://digest.bps.org.uk/2015/01/the-psy-chology-of-facebook-digested.html) for a very thorough consideration of a wide and varied literature around Facebook users. One reason that Facebook has become so popular among Western societies might stem from the diverse activities offered by the website. Popularity. Already, this description of SNSs shows that personal preference for communication will influence how one portrays the self on such websites. Facebook may be the SNS with the least narrow focus of behaviour and expression of personal identities and associated personality characteristics. Prior to exploring the role of personality traits and individual differences on impression management on Facebook in particular, we shall digress to consider how self-presentation differs by virtue of the social media engaged via other websites.

3.2.1   Social media

If you enter the term "most popular social networking sites in the world" into an online search engine, a very western biased list emerges that usually includes, in no particular order, *Facebook, Twitter, Instagram, Pinterest* and *LinkedIn*. Each of these SNSs uses different formats and different ways of broadcasting the self to the world and can all be categorised as falling under the umbrella term *social media*. Whereas Twitter confines an individual to 140 characters per message, Instagram is a photo and video sharing SNS. LinkedIn, on the other hand, is a networking site for professional connections that thrives on linking people with similar work interests, promoting themselves, their achievements and their connections to like-minded others. It is surely a massive undertaking to establish consistent relationships of personality and self-presentation across all of these different types of SNS, especially as each type in itself promotes a different type of presentation. Although this might reflect an accurate statement of difficulty in establishing links across diverse types of social media, the outline of the actual self in Chapter 2 and of the core self earlier in this chapter suggested that those characteristics and traits which create the core consistent component of one's self should be evident regardless of temporal and situational differences. It could therefore be expected that a person displays consistent characteristics irrespective of which SNS is being used.

Another difficulty thrown into this mix is that the recipients of communication across the diverse social media sites are likely somewhat

DOI: 10.1057/9781137483416.0005

different. Posting pictures of your drunken summer holiday to Facebook might portray your actual self of an extravert party-loving fun individual to your friends and family, but you would unlikely post these to LinkedIn or ResearchGate. You would (hopefully) be more likely to post a respect-able business-like portrait image of yourself to these types of website. This does not suggest that you are portraying two different people. Both of these images reflect who you really are, but you would be selecting those aspects of your actual self that are most relevant to the type of social media in which you are engaging. Thus, people may use different types of social media and SNS relating to different features of their self in a flexible goal-directed manner, a manner which allows for a continuous creation, editing and recreation of the cyberself depending upon the task in hand.

This line of reasoning is akin to the premises of Uses and Gratifications (U&G) Theory (see Section 2.4), but whether this theory could explain possible differences in self-presentation across diverse social media sites based upon the goals and needs would depend upon whether the intended goals are actually achieved. There are some examples of attempts to employ U&G theory to understanding the diverse motives that people have for using Facebook. For example, while some people use SNSs to develop or maintain relationships, others use them purely for entertainment purposes (e.g., Sheldon, 2008a, 2008b; Special & Li-Barber, 2012). How self-presentation on SNSs is manipulated will play into how these different types of goal are achieved. Conversely, the level of self-information that people feel able to disclose online could influence the goals that people seek from their online disclosures. In line with this notion, Tosun (2012) found that the likelihood of establishing new relationships online was linked to peoples' perceived ability to share their true or real self online. Further support for a uses and gratifications approach to understanding self-presentations on Facebook is offered in Smock's (2011) identification of nine motives that people report for using Facebook: *relaxing, entertainment, expressive information sharing, escapism, companionship, professional advancement, social interaction, habitual passing of time* and *meeting new people*. There are thus a variety of motivations and reasons as to why people use SNSs. Some may use them to create and maintain relationships, while others might use them as a form of self-expression or as a tool for learning (Hew, 2011; Special & Li-Barber, 2012; Tosun, 2012). Regardless of how or why people use SNSs, they require a certain level of self-representation.

DOI: 10.1057/9781137483416.0005

There is some evidence to suggest that individuals present themselves slightly differently on SNSs to how they present themselves in the offline world. Using the Big Five personality dimensions Gosling, Gaddis and Vazire (2007) found, for example, that individuals displayed a dissociation between their online and offline personality profiles. In a study among students, Hew (2011) found that people were likely to represent their actual self on SNSs since any false information would be quickly found out by people who knew them both offline and online. This fits with a Warranting Theory approach to understanding social media use, since SNSs offer a useful verification tool for establishing that people are conveying their actual self in their online presentations (see Section 2.5). Hew's findings are however contrary to a demonstration by Gibbs, Ellison and Heino (2006) that people tend to be somewhat creative with their cyberself. It is worth bearing in mind that in 2006, a notion of anonymity prevailed in online behaviours with SNSs being in their infancy. By 2011, it might be assumed that people are far more aware of the consequences of misrepresenting themselves online, especially on SNSs where this information is shared with at least some people with whom they likely interact offline. This is demonstrated in recent research which suggested that security concerns are causing Facebook users to become more reluctant in the sharing of their personal information on Facebook disclosures (Wilson, Gosling & Graham 2012). This section has made reference to both the U&G theory and warranting theory while providing a brief consideration of the interplay of personality factors and self-presentation on SNSs. Both of these theories were however designed to explain offline behaviour in an Internet-less era. Very few new theories have been designed to explain how people self-present online, but one that has garnered recent interest, the dual-factor model of motivations and human belonging, will now be considered in more detail. In addition to the nine motives identified by Smock (2011), the use of Facebook has been associated with a number of further motivations, including a boost to self-esteem (Gonzales & Hancock, 2011; Steinfield, Ellison & Lampe, 2008) and enhancing social connectedness (Sheldon, Abad & Hirsch, 2011). While the latter is similar to Smock's motivation of *social interaction*, the boost to self-esteem appears to be distinct from Smock's nine motivations. Oftentimes it is difficult to create a coherent theory that would be able to take such an array of motivations into consideration in a consistent and predictive manner. If the nine motivations were organised, then they could possibly fall under the more broader terms of

DOI: 10.1057/9781137483416.0005

leisure and entertainment and *relationships*. Or, they might be simply categorised as *professional* and *personal* motivations. Regardless of the label given, future research might want to consider how these motivations could be grouped according to the desired outcome that each motivation aims to achieve. For instance, the desired outcome of *social interaction* could be to achieve a new romantic relationship, or it could be to connect with like-minded people offline.

3.3   Dual-factor model of motivations and human belonging

One model that has attempted to use just two motivations to explain Facebook use was offered in a recent paper by Nadkarni and Hoffmann (2012). They proposed a *dual-factor model* of Facebook use, whereby individuals use the SNS to fulfil the basic human needs of *belonging* and *self-presentation*. Facebook particularly lends itself to self-presentation through the use of different types of content, from photos to basic self-descriptive information (Zhao, Grasmuck & Martin, 2008). As human beings we have a basic need to belong (Baumeister & Leary, 1995). Early research suggested that this need could be met through the use of social media, especially if it is not being met offline. Social networking site profiles offer a good opportunity to present the self in a way that is reflective of the real self, yet flexible enough to test different aspects of the self. Seidman (2013) reports on two ways in which individuals use Facebook to achieve this sense of belonging, namely *information-seeking* and *communication*. Though the former sees the user as obtaining information about others from the SNS, communication reflects the individual's need to share personal information to connect with others. Seidman goes on to elaborate on two motives that underlie these behaviours, the belongingness motive of *acceptance-seeking* and the motive of *connecting* with others. These motives underlie the presentational behaviours of how people generally share factual information about themselves and their emotional state of mind along with their psychological well-being. One particular way in which posters to SNSs achieve the connectedness that provides a sense of belonging is to engage in attention-seeking behaviours or those that involve presenting aspects of the hidden or ideal self. Seidman (2013) tested the dual-factor model relating to the Big Five personality traits and individuals' Facebook use in order to meet self-presentation

DOI: 10.1057/9781137483416.0005

and belonging needs. In terms of achieving a sense of belongingness, people who are highly agreeable and/or neurotic appear to use social media to meet this need. Seidman suggests that this may be because they are not meeting this need in their offline world, possibly due to the difficulties they experience in socialising. Highly neurotic individuals were also most likely to engage in controlled self-presentation online, as were highly conscientious participants. The Internet may thus afford an individual the opportunity to express aspects of their offline self in a safe environment, which helps achieve the goal of human belonging. Seidman (2013) concludes that the dual-factor model fits with a goal-directed tool approach to understanding how some individuals create the cyberself based on the underlying motivations of satisfying basic human needs. It thus adds to a uses and gratifications approach by offering an explanation of the motivations that drive the user to achieve the gratifications. A final consideration in terms of motivational self-presentations is given in this chapter by returning to underlying individual characteristics that may drive online impression management.

3.4   Loneliness, social anxiety and depression

Early studies of the role of personality in online interactions focused on traits associated with offline social withdrawal, such as loneliness, depression and social anxiety. *Loneliness* is often experienced in the absence of social interaction. It can create a very emotional sense of the self being unwanted or rejected by society or those to whom the person wishes to feel connected and close. Feeling as if one does not belong can be an underlying cause of *social anxiety*. Social anxiety arises when a person feels extremely uncomfortable to the point of psychological distress at the thought of interacting with other people. It is often associated with a fear of being judged by others and an increased sense of insecurity. Whereas this is psychological discomfort directed at the specific act of social interaction, *depression* can be more generalised. The simplest definition of depression revolves around having low mood, feeling lethargic and not wanting to interact with others. This book is not aimed at understanding these psychological facets of human behaviour, but is merely using these as an illustration of three connected emotions and feelings that can result in a person not feeling able to engage in offline social activities. Given this assumption about loneliness, social anxiety

DOI: 10.1057/9781137483416.0005

and depression, it is understandable that early cyberpsychology research focused on (1) how these people might compensate their offline social worlds through online interactions and (2) tried to use these online interactions to understand the social side of the Internet.

The early research around these three aspects of personality produced mixed findings, but one of the early and consistent notions to emerge was that individuals experiencing symptoms of loneliness and social anxiety could use the Internet to their advantage, to express their actual self (e.g., McKenna, Green & Gleason, 2002; Scharlott & Christ, 1995). Research evidence to support this notion followed with demonstrations that some people use the Internet as a social compensation tool to create a social existence online that they may be missing offline (e.g., Peter, Valkenburg & Schouten, 2005; Tosun & Lajunen, 2010). This early work thus demonstrated that people displaying certain individual characteristics may be more or less likely to use the Internet to suit their personalities. This line of reasoning fits with the premises of U&G theory (Katz, Blumler & Gurevitch, 1973). It illustrates how people could use the Internet to satisfy a basic human need that they feel is not met offline. In this instance that need may be one of social belonging.

More recent research has also reported a role of loneliness in online behaviours with Aykut Ceyhan and Ceyhan (2008) reporting that among a sample of 559 Turkish students, loneliness was the most important predictor of problematic Internet use with depression a close second predictor. Another important observation comes from Kim, LaRose and Wei (2009) who found that both lonely and depressed participants were more likely to develop strong compulsive Internet use, but this Internet use did not increase their sense of loneliness. This would suggest that it is indeed the characteristics of loneliness and depression which are driving the Internet use, rather than use of the Internet creating a sense of loneliness and depression in those participants, a finding echoed by Lee and Stapinski's (2011) demonstration that social anxiety appeared to be a significant predictor of problematic Internet use among 338 participants. These authors suggested that using the Internet offers the socially anxious some sense of control over their actions and a reduced risk of negative evaluations. Further evidence to support the notion that personality traits drive one's online self-presentations rather than the reverse was offered in an early account of depression-related Internet use based on the suggestion that reactive depression could evolve from a sense of inability to control stressors that influence one's quality of life

DOI: 10.1057/9781137483416.0005

and thereby one's notion of self (LaRose, Eastin & Gregg, 2001). Rose and colleagues tested 171 students and found no direct link between Internet use and depression. What they did find, however, was that people displaying symptoms of depression used the Internet to seek support in a way that reduced their depressive feelings. This, again, fits with a goal-directed uses and gratifications view of how peoples' notion of self, in this instance led by certain traits and emotions, leads a person to behave in a way online that meets their needs. It is, however, rare that these individual tendencies of depression, social anxiety and loneliness operate in (1) complete separation from one another, (2) complete isolation from other personality traits such as extraversion or shyness and (3) complete isolation from external factors.

3.5   Shyness and self-esteem

Shyness and self-esteem are not necessarily associated with social withdrawal, although both can lead to withdrawing from social interactions and are often associated with depression, social anxiety and loneliness. These personality factors have also drawn much research interest over the last couple of decades as they can be very influential in how people go about their social interactions. People who are *shy* often experience high levels of physical and psychological discomfort, awkwardness and apprehension when around other people, especially if they do not know those people. Sometimes the levels of shyness experienced are so severe that they can cause social anxiety and complete social withdrawal. One's level of self-esteem can also be affected by, and affects, shyness. *Self-esteem* is one's overall positive or negative evaluation of the self as a worthy human being. It is not to be confused with *self-efficacy* which refers to a person's level of perceived ability to complete tasks and goals in life. Rather than listing all previous research in this area, a couple of select findings that illustrate the difficulty in disentangling the different personality factors and their role in impression management are outlined. If you are interested in finding out more about these characteristics and other aspects of personality touched upon in this chapter, Dr Chris Fullwood offers an excellent overview in the book *Cyberpsychology* (Attrill, 2015).

Shyness is often linked with personality traits that convey reduced liking of social interactions, such as introversion. Many of the factors that cause a person to feel shy or socially anxious in offline situations are not

DOI: 10.1057/9781137483416.0005

present online. For example, the fear of immediate social humiliation or rejection (Pennebaker, 1989) is especially absent in asynchronous online communications. Moreover, the opportunity to craft carefully constructed text responses in asynchronous communications allows the shy individual to think about a possible outcome of the communication and construct it to avoid social embarrassment, the biggest fear that hinders their offline interactions. To avoid isolation or loneliness, and to ensure that the basic human need of belonging is met, Davis and Kraus (1989) proposed that these individuals engage in *social compensation*. According to these researchers, people seek to meet their basic human needs that are not being met offline by using media to create the need fulfilment. In terms of the Internet, McKenna, Green and Gelason (2002) suggested that people who feel inhibited offline could use the Internet to create a sense of social belonging. After all, the Internet is awash with applications and websites that offer interactions with multiple others that would simply not be possible offline. In support of the *social compensation hypothesis*, Lee, Moore, Park and Park (2012) recently observed that participants with lower levels of self-reported self-esteem have more friends on Facebook than those with higher reported self-esteem. Interactions with those friends and the sharing of self-information are, however, often characterised by negative communications (Forest & Wood, 2012), which is not surprising given that low self-esteem reflects a negative evaluation of the self. Therefore, although shy people might be using the Internet to compensate socially, their online communications appear to reflect their actual or true self.

The *social enhancement hypothesis* is often cited as reflecting the converse to the social compensation hypothesis, namely that people act out online the same level of social interaction that they have offline to maintain their social existence (e.g., Valkenburg, Schouten & Peter, 2005). Papacharissi and Mendelson (2011) also suggest that those socially active offline can better take advantage of online opportunities to connect with multiple others. Although there is some evidence that suggests this to be the case (e.g., Hampton, Goulet, Rainie & Purcell, 2011), of importance here is that regardless of level of self-esteem and levels of offline social interaction, people appear to consistently present the self online as they do offline. The person who displays low self-esteem offline presents negatively online, and the offline extravert seeks to enhance their social life online. Although evidence to support this proposal is also offered in demonstrations of SNSs being used to both accept others and develop

DOI: 10.1057/9781137483416.0005

relationships (Yu, Tian, Vogel & Kwok, 2010), some people report using SNSs as a method for dealing with their feelings of social rejection and disconnect (Sheldon, Abad & Hirsch, 2011). Research thus offers no definitive answer as yet as to the role of self-esteem in online impression management, with the possible exception of a recent paper by Marriott and Buchanan (2014) demonstrating that levels of introversion are associated with higher levels of self-expression online than offline.

3.6   Naïve psychologies and pop-personalities

This chapter has focused on the role that individual characteristics and traits play in how people present themselves online. Chapter 4 considers the way in which peoples' levels of sharing information about the self are affected by, and affect, the ways in which they present the cyberself. This chapter closes, however, with a consideration aimed at promoting thinking about the Internet as a tool that anyone and everyone can now use to analyse and interpret others' self-presentations, the naïve psychologist approach to the Internet.

One of the features of the Internet that has enabled it to become the everyday tool now used by so many people is its wide accessibility and affordability. Its ease of use also sees it coming full circle of Heider's (1958) naïve psychologist theory. Heider proposed that all humans are lay psychologists who attempt to piece together overt and covert clues to understand their own and others' behaviour. This laid the foundation for a number of subsequent attribution theories which proposed variations on how diverse external and internal cues are used to piece together inferences about the causes of behaviour (e.g., Kelley's (1967) Covariation Model or Bem's (1972) Theory of Self-Perception). If you enter the search term "psychology of Facebook users" into an online search engine, for example, it will return a number of newspaper and pop-psychology posts before it even considers returning an academic article. Indeed, in a post in the Daily Telegraph in June 2014, the *FiveLabs* personality analyser (http://labs.five.com/) was discussed which allows people to analyse their one personality based upon their Facebook posts. The question, or possible concern, that arises from this is one of academic and scientific information being used by untrained people. If an individual runs an analysis on his/her profile and it suggests that s/he is 90% neurotic, what should s/he do with that information? Of what

DOI: 10.1057/9781137483416.0005

use is it outside of a more appropriate context? Indeed, it could lead to negative self-fulfilling assumptions that are used to reinforce a negative or anxious self-image. This is just one example of many such "tools" that are increasing in popularity on the Internet, to the point of many users considering themselves knowledgeable in interpreting and analysing others' posts. You might like to ponder these questions for a while and consider how psychology should move forward with the dissemination of research findings that could be inappropriately used.

DOI: 10.1057/9781137483416.0005

4
Motivations for Sharing the Cyberself

Abstract: *One of the main features of online self-presentation is the way in which people use selective and controlled self-disclosures to share information about the self to create certain self-images to others. This chapter explores this notion by considering the motivations outlined in Chapter 3 as underlying motivations that influence the way in which self-disclosure ensues online. Also considered are a number of factors that influence this motivated self-presentation, including reciprocal interactions, voluntary and involuntary self-disclosures.*

Key words: human belonging; motivations; reciprocity; self-disclosure; voluntary and involuntary disclosures

Attrill, Alison. *The Manipulation of Online Self-Presentation: Create, Edit, Re-edit and Present.* Basingstoke: Palgrave Macmillan, 2015. DOI: 10.1057/9781137483416.0006.

In Chapters 2 and 3, the idea was touched upon that underlying motivations of human behaviour drive the ways in which people present themselves online. The overarching theme that has been presented in the preceding chapters revolved around peoples' personality traits and individual characteristics being associated with their creation of an actual, ideal or ought self online that resembles their true offline self. The conceptualisation that has overwhelmingly been used thus far to illustrate these considerations is one based loosely on Uses and Gratifications (U&G) theory (Katz, Blumler & Gurevitch, 1973) combined with peoples' motivations driving their online self-presentation in a goal-directed manner. Most of the activities that people carry out in this goal-driven manner require that they share information about themselves online. The focus of this chapter is to consider how the motivations that drive online self-presentation use the process of sharing self-information in order to achieve the sought behavioural goal. It begins by considering human motivations and drives in a little more detail before elaborating upon some of the most important factors that impact online self-disclosures, the sharing of self-information online.

4.1   Motivations

Throughout this section, I would like you to think about your own reasons for engaging in online interactions. Think about how you reveal information about yourself online and what are the goals of those revelations. For example, some people might reveal information on Facebook because they are feeling sad and want cheering up. Others might use self-revelation as a cathartic release for their feelings of anger and hurt. These are motivated behaviours. Offline, we are often aware of why we engage in certain behaviours or activities, but online the motivations for our behaviours might not always be so clear. This section outlines how classic offline research is being adopted and adapted to understand the motivations and drives underlying online behaviours, especially those that lead to online interactions and relationships.

There are many ways in which we can approach the understanding of human behaviour. Social Psychology, for instance, focuses on the environmental and societal impact upon the individual's learned behaviours, whereas Goffman's (1959) sociological view saw people constructing their daily lives in a way which incorporates a positive image of the self to

DOI: 10.1057/9781137483416.0006

others. From a Biological Personality perspective, humans are a product of nature rather than the nurture of their social surroundings. Although these views may all differ in *how* humans *acquire* given behavioural tendencies and whether these are dispositional or situational, nearly all approaches to understanding the human psyche and behaviour suggest that overt behaviour is driven by internal processes such as basic motivations and drives. An excellent starting point for understanding the role of such motivations in online behaviour is to borrow a theory from Personality Psychology.

In his now classic Theory of Human Motivation, Maslow (1943) proposed a hierarchy of human needs that drive behaviour with the ultimate satisfaction being one of *self-actualisation*. The bottom-most layer of his hierarchical pyramid consisted of *physiological needs*, above which lies the need for *safety*. Once these needs have been met, a human strives for the next layer of needs which is that of *love and belonging*. These then feed into esteem and ultimately *self-actualisation*. People strive to satisfy the primary physiological needs such as hunger and thirst before fulfilling those that are more of a psychological nature. One of these is the layer of love/belonging, which has been further expanded upon as a key motivation that drives human interaction both offline and online. Maslow did not purport all needs to be consciously considered before seeking satisfaction of this need. Rather, behaviour may be driven towards a need without awareness or understanding of the necessity to meet that need. Of interest for the current discussion is Maslow's suggestion of the necessity to experience belongingness and feel loved, without which one may struggle to achieve ultimate self-actualisation. Over the years there have been numerous theories which have honed in on this basic human need to suggest it to be a fundamental motivation or drive of human behaviour. While Bowlby (e.g., 1969, 1973) suggested that humans need to create and maintain social bonds, for example, Baumeister and Leary (1995) put forward the proposal of *human belongingness*. According to Baumeister and Leary, all humans have the fundamental and basic need to create significant and lasting relationships in a way that makes them feel wanted, liked and as if they are connected to other human beings. To achieve this, people engage in frequent positive interactions that create stability and foster further interactions with those people to whom they wish to feel connected. Motivation to achieve this sense of belongingness is driven by affective, cognitive and behavioural consequences that lead

DOI: 10.1057/9781137483416.0006

the individual to feel like s/he belongs within a given social interaction or relationship(s). These relationships can be of either a romantic, platonic or group nature. According to all of these conceptualisations, should a human being not achieve a sense of belonging s/he could experience an array of negative cognitive, affective and behavioural consequences (see Baumeister & Leary, 1995 for a fuller overview of these conceptualisations).

4.2   Human-belongingness and the Internet

Based on a motivations approach to understanding human behaviour, people may create and manipulate their self-presentations in a way that fosters gratification of this need for belonging. Whereas once this process of impression management in order to achieve that gratification would have required time and progress among chosen relationships offline (see e.g., Sternberg, 1986), the opportunity for instant gratification of many human needs via an ever-connected Internet means that people can achieve this sense of belonging almost instantaneously. Moreover, they likely create and manipulate versions of the self in a way that enhances and provokes instant responses to meet such needs. This, once again, takes us back to Turkle's (1995) notion that people can play around with their cyberselves to explore different self-identities online. People might thus use the Internet in a goal-directed manner to find acceptance for a certain version of the self that may not be welcomed in their offline social networks. Consider, for example, a person who for a large portion of his/her life has downplayed a certain aspect of his/her core self for the sake of social acceptance offline. Online, s/he might make this part of the self his/her core cyberself, the aspect that draws attention and receives acceptance in a chosen online environment. This could be considered to be a goal-directed manipulation of self-presentation that might cause fractions in one's self-image or self-perception, almost like living out different lives. However, if people could achieve the desired sense of acceptance and belonging from their manipulated self-presentations, then their cyberself and online interactions could subsequently become more important than their offline interactions. In other words, while achieving the positive sense of belonging online, a detrimental side effect could be a diminished existence either online or offline as has been outlined by Walther's (1996) Hyperpersonal Communications

DOI: 10.1057/9781137483416.0006

Theory (see Section 2.3). This could then create offline social withdrawal and associated psychological issues that would suggest the seeking out of self-acceptance and social belonging online to be a negative feature of Internet use.

One other feature of Baumeister and Leary's (1995) theory that needs consideration before assuming the Internet to be either a positive or negative tool used for meeting human needs is the time-frame of acquiring social acceptance online. These authors suggest that the sense of belonging that humans crave is built up over a period of prolonged interactions based on shared experiences and intimacies, rather than instantaneously through a few shared clicks and exchanges online. In order to achieve a sense of belonging via computer-mediated communication (CMC), people would need to engage in repeated and frequent communications to foster the prolonged interaction. Consider online dating as an example. There are many reasons that an individual might create a profile on an online dating website. For the purposes of this exercise, let us assume that they are doing so because they want to meet a new romantic partner. Initially, they will create a version of self that paints them, in their eyes, in the best possible light, maybe even a creation of their ideal self. As they receive communication from potential partners and subsequently engage in repeated exchanges, they will likely reveal more and more of their actual self to these people. These exchanges could thus see the prolonged and repeated communications help result in a sense of belonging or acceptance of whichever self they have chosen to present to those potential partners. The question that arises from this consideration is whether that sense of belonging online can be equated to the sense of belonging that Baumeister and Leary suggested to occur offline. Until such point that a relationship has been transferred to, and successfully exists offline, one might perceive the interactions to be less real than offline social bonds. This is of course conjecture, given that the goals of the online daters would surely determine their perceptions of how real their online interactions are. It might also depend on how consistent they are with their self-revelations and their presentations of their real or actual self online, given that this self would very quickly become evident in any future offline interaction. Regardless of whether online interactions are considered real or able to satisfy basic human needs, in order to even attempt such gratification, people need to reveal some self-information online to create even a notion of acceptance and belonging. It is this process of self-disclosure that may provide the key

DOI: 10.1057/9781137483416.0006

to establishing the type of lasting exchanges featured in Baumeister and Leary's theory.

4.3   Self-disclosure

The first definition of the term *self-disclosure* was offered by Jourard (1971) to describe the revelation of information about the self to another person or persons. It occurs both offline and online when an individual shares any type of self-information with other people (e.g., Wheeless, 1978; Wheeless & Grotz, 1976). The term self-disclosure has also been used to describe self-presentation, but for the purposes of this text, it will be used as intended by Jourard (1971). When considering how people self-disclose offline, general self- disclosure is often represented by the *depth* and *breadth* of the self-information shared. The depth refers to how personal and intimate information is, while breadth refers to the broadness of the information being shared (Wheeless, 1978). Not that many years ago, an individual's self-disclosures would have occurred only offline, possibly to a select few people within easy geographical reach. Exceptions might be the exchanges that took place via written letters, telephone or even telegraph communications (e.g., Standage, 1998). Offline self-disclosure has been assessed in a variety of ways for an array of communications, ranging from verbal exchanges that serve to maintain interpersonal relationships (e.g., Giles, Coupland & Coupland, 1991; Petronio, Martin & Littlefield, 1984), handwritten letters and telephone conversations (e.g., Petronio & Bradford, 1993; Shulman, Seiffge-Krenke & Dimitrovsky, 1994) before self-disclosures being considered in online spheres.

Even 25 years ago, it would have been difficult to consider how such work on self-disclosure might be comparable to the masses of online communication engaged in nowadays. Although once people may have resisted the use of new technologies, it appears that people have readily accepted using the Internet for communication purposes and at first glance, at least, it further appears that people are happy to share self-information across the wide and varied modes of CMC available. As Attrill (2012a, p. 4) notes "Friendships, romances, one off sexual liaisons, gaming interactions, advice and even counselling are but a few of the human encounters that are now being brokered online, sometimes without individuals ever meeting in their comparative offline worlds" (Yum

DOI: 10.1057/9781137483416.0006

& Hara, 2006). It is thus not surprising that these powers of connecting to people the world over have brought with them comparisons of online and offline self-disclosures. One consideration often overlooked however is that online self-disclosures might evoke manipulations or variations on self-presentation that were highly unlikely in offline interactions. Let us illustrate this with an example. In a lecture this week, a student quite happily discussed how she had befriended a person online with whom she frequently games. She has been communicating with him for more than five years, yet only knows his user tag, not his name, real identity or really his actual location, simply a chosen name that he uses to represent himself online. He could be anyone – He simply chooses to represent himself in this way online. Yet, they frequently discuss the goings on of their daily lives and communicate as well-known friends. There is a level and type of self-disclosure here that is not reliant on knowing each others' real self-identities. Some might find this type of interaction a little strange, but this is becoming a more acceptable way of communicating with others for many people, and by doing so, it brings with it a whole area of self-representation and self-disclosure online that simply cannot be equalled offline. Indeed, much early work that compared online to offline self-disclosures supported that people were often likely to share more self-information, and more intimate and personal information online with people who are completely unknown to one another in the offline world (e.g., Christofides, Muise & Desmarais, 2009; Gibbs, Ellison & Heino, 2006; Bonebrake, 2002; Cooper & Sportolari, 1997). Sharing the self online in this way was initially considered to result from a sense of anonymity online affording individuals the ability to explore their self-identity in a way that avoided the social humiliation or social rejection that they might have experienced in an offline encounter (McKenna & Bargh, 1998).

To further consider whether people do expose themselves so willingly online, this chapter explores some of the research associated with how people present themselves online through their online self-disclosures. Throughout this text, consideration has been given to whether people are more likely to present their actual self online, or a carefully crafted version of self that represents an ideal who they would like to be. In terms of self-disclosure, some evidence suggests that people are more likely to reveal their real or actual self to others as a relationship develops (e.g., Chelune, 1979; Greene, Derlega & Mathews, 2006). This gradual revelation of the true self is the premise of one of the founding theories of offline

DOI: 10.1057/9781137483416.0006

self-disclosure, the Social Penetration Theory (SPT) (Altman & Taylor, 1973). According to SPT, people build up a relationship by exchanging self-information in a progressive manner. The next time someone asks you your name and you return that information, think about their response. They will likely tell you their name. What subsequently follows may be an exchange between you of very basic demographic information, such as where you are from and what you do for a living. As your conversation progresses over time, SPT would predict that you share more personal and intimate information with one another. Altman and Taylor liken this to the layers of an onion that are gradually peeled back until you reach the core central information about your self, that really deep and mean-ingful information that you only share with those closest and dearest to you. Thus, the longer and more in-depth communications become, the more people are likely to reveal their real self (e.g., Gibbs et al., 2006). That said, not all relationships are destined to become close and intimate. People hold various different types of relationships which might differ in their intensity and levels of personal information shared. In this instance, self-presentation is very much constructed and gauged according to the goal in hand, the goal of forming a certain type of relationship for which self-information is shared accordingly (see also Attrill, 2012a.). If online self-disclosure is considered in this goal-directed manner, not only does it follow that it is used to present the self in a carefully constructed manner online, but also that there is possibly some motivational aspect to using self-disclosures in this manner.

To understand the role of motivations in guiding online self-disclosures, consideration is once again given to the dual factor model of online communications (Nadkarni & Hoffmann, 2012). According to this model, people use the Internet to meet the basic human needs of belonging and self-presentation. Self-disclosure is used to present the self in a certain way online. Therefore, self-disclosure could be considered to be one of the tools used in the motivation of self-presentation. Moreover, the basic action of self-disclosing uses the information-seeking and communication modes reportedly associated with the two basic human needs (Seidman, 2013). In order to obtain information about another individual, a person may need to share self-information online in an ongoing communication. In fact, on considering further motives offered by Seidman as underlying online self-presentations, self-disclosure is most often directed at creating a connection with others that results in a form of acceptance. Support for this line of reasoning comes from

DOI: 10.1057/9781137483416.0006

Davis (2012), who demonstrated that one of the underlying motivations of online communication for adolescents is to self-disclose information that helps create a sense of belonging. Among 2079 participants who completed a questionnaire, backed up with interview data from 32 participants in the age group of 13–18 years, Davis found that by disclosing information about the self via various forms of CMC (e.g., Facebook, instant messaging and texting), participants maintained a sense of belonging to their friends. Of interest is also Davis' finding that public posts on Facebook led participants to feel as if they were connecting with their wider peer group. Self-disclosure may thus provide the tool with which people create and manipulate their self-presentations with the aim of gratifying basic human needs.

4.3.1 The Internet shield and freedom of self-expression

The material outlined thus far relating to online self-disclosure could be interpreted as suggesting a somewhat footloose and fancy-free interpretation of peoples' use of their self-information online. There are a number of possible reasons as to why early research found that online disclosures ensued quicker than offline disclosures (e.g., Leung, 2002). When communicating online, people might perceive the Internet as providing them with a barrier, almost like a shield that protects them from immediate retorts and provides them with a seeming freedom of self-expression. Consider your own online communications and whether you might self-disclose from behind this shield in a very gradual manner, testing the waters of acceptance or validation of your thoughts and feelings, your notions of self-image, self-efficacy and self-esteem when building any type of relationship online. Alternatively, you may use the Internet to splurge your innermost thoughts. It could be the case that there are factors which affect your own levels of self-disclosure, including who you are talking to (reciprocity), how you are talking to them (mode of communication) and the type of relationship you wish to establish with them.

4.4 Factors influencing online self-disclosure

4.4.1 Reciprocity

The word *communication* comes from the Latin word *commūnicāre*, which means to share. Thus, by the very virtue of its meaning, online

DOI: 10.1057/9781137483416.0006

communication involves sharing some type of information. Given the focus of this text on self-presentation online, rather than exploring online communication *per se* interest lies in understanding how information exchanges shape and are shaped by the contributors' presentation of self. The first consideration is given to those people who receive the shared information, the communication recipient(s) or partner(s) (CR/CPs). Initially, much of the work that considered self-creation online via self-disclosure focused on the discloser rather than on whom one is sharing information with. When constructing online communications, the intended CR will likely influence how a person represents themselves in that communication. Consider for instance two separate emails that you might send. If you are replying to an advertisement for a job, then you should not begin the email with "Hey Dude ..." but with appropriate job application etiquette. Conversely, if you are sending your parents an email from your travels abroad, you would unlikely open it with "Dear Sir/Madam ..." but would likely use a more relaxed form of address.

The CRs play a large role in how people receive justification and verification for the presented self online. Work by Moon (2000) demonstrated this idea in its most basic form by showing that simply having a computer introduce itself by name to participants led to these participants sharing more information than those who did not receive the computer introduction. That people more freely share information if they feel that they are receiving something from others in return was also demonstrated by Rollman, Krug and Parente (2000). They considered online chat room exchanges in which the length of a communication response positively correlated to how much self-information was subsequently disclosed. It may not be the actual content of information shared by a CR that determines how one responds or what information one subsequently shares, but simply the fact that someone is perceived to be interested in the information that is being shared. In other words, it may not be the type or length of information that is disclosed, but the perceived reciprocal process of sharing information that is important (Joinson, 2001). This is in line with the notion of gradual self-disclosure expressed in Altman and Taylor's (1973) SPT as well as with demonstrations that people exchange superficial self-information rather than splurging their innermost thoughts and feelings (e.g., Attrill & Jalil, 2011). It is almost as if people feel compelled to offer self-information in response to information provided by a CR. During an online interaction, every time a person reveals self-information, a CR might feel that they have to match

DOI: 10.1057/9781137483416.0006

the disclosure. According to the Warranting Theory (Walther & Parks 2002; Walther, 2011), it might be proposed that the more validated and accurate a person perceives self-disclosures to be of another's real self, the more likely they might be to match that self-disclosure. This is an interesting proposal as to how warranting may play a role in the use of self-disclosure to entice revelations of the real self from a communications partner that would benefit from future research.

4.4.2   Mode of communication, voluntary and involuntary disclosures

How people choose to share different aspects of their self online may be dependent upon which mode of communication they are using. Some forms of online communication are more private than others. If sharing aspects of the self via a status update on Facebook, for instance, a person might be more conservative in opinions and views that could reflect their real self as this is less private than instant messaging. In other words, people may conceal information about the true self due to concerns as to whether the mode of communication is private. Self-disclosure has been shown to be linked to impression management and the desire for a positive image of self via *self-concealment*. This occurs when people actively suppress negative personal information (Larson & Chastain, 1990; Uysal, Lin & Knee, 2010). The notion of self-concealment also links with the idea of presenting oneself in the best possible light to achieve a sense of belonging and connectedness. People who score high on self-concealment scales often display higher levels of anxiety-related feelings and emotions (e.g., Kahn & Hessling, 2001). Using a very public mode of communication could heighten these feelings, with high concealers thus choosing more private and personal modes usually employed for one-to-one exchanges rather than broadcasting the self to multiple others. This raises an interesting question as an avenue for future research, namely whether people who broadcast themselves to the masses are broadcasting their real self. Although no specific statistics could be found about successful comedians, comedic actors and actors who suffer from depression, there does appear to be a high number of these who at some point or other report that they suffer from depression or depression-like symptoms. Considering this in light of the current discussion, it could be the case that they use the stage to broadcast a more up-beat psychologically healthy version of themselves. It is thus feasible that this is also what some people may be doing when using YouTube and other

DOI: 10.1057/9781137483416.0006

self-broadcasting technologies. Online, people may actively choose to conceal certain aspects of their self for fear of social rejection or negative reactions when using public broadcasting methods, or even those that are intended at more than a handful of recipients. The mode of communication used for interpersonal exchanges online has been shown to be important across an array of online self-disclosure studies. For instance, Barack and Gluck-Ofri (2007) demonstrated that the quantity and type of self-information shared online is influenced by the type of webpage on which the exchange takes place. Instant messaging services have also been shown to lead to heightened sharing of intimate self-details (Leung, 2002). Continuing with a motivations and needs-based interpretation of how people create the self online, choosing the appropriate mode of communication to self-disclose and achieve a representation of a certain self to single or multiple others seems important.

4.5   Voluntary and involuntary self-disclosure

A project reported by Attrill and Jalil (2011; Attrill 2012b) discussed among other factors exactly this notion of different types of Internet arena fostering and promoting different ways and goals of sharing self-information online. They noted that self-disclosure initially occurs only for superficial self-information rather than the splurge of one's entire self-detail. The follow up study by Attrill (2012b) demonstrated that in addition to sharing only superficial self-information online, there were significant differences among the types of self-information shared on shopping, instant messaging and social networking websites as well as in general online communications (i.e., email). The study was carried out using Magno's (2009) self-disclosure scale to measure five categories of self-information: *personal matters, interests, intimate feelings, beliefs* and *relationships*. Although the sharing of intimate feelings and beliefs was significantly less than the other three categories of self-information via the types of communication in which self-information is freely and voluntarily disclosed (instant messaging, social networking and general communication), the sharing on shopping websites was very superficial and akin to a needs-based type of sharing. When completing any registration for any type of website, a person usually has to disclose some personal details. Attrill (2012b) refers to this as *involuntary self-disclosure*, a needs-must sharing of information to achieve a desired goal. This

DOI: 10.1057/9781137483416.0006

information is factual and reflects a person's actual self. Using the example of an online dating website, in order to create a profile, information about the real self needs to be shared (involuntary self-disclosure) before proceeding to revealing that information which the poster wants to use for the purposes of impression management (voluntary self-disclosure). All of your *voluntary* self-disclosures, such as the information about you and your life that you freely share on any Internet arena is exactly that – voluntary. It is information that you are selectively choosing to disclose, possibly in a way that manipulates how the recipients or respondents of that information will perceive and respond to your sharing. People may engage in involuntary sharing of personal details online for several reasons. That is, they may need to share personal details to achieve a certain goal online, including the instant gratification of purchasing desired goods or becoming a member of a given online or offline society. This is the type of information that is often retained by the Internet site and could potentially be used by them or third parties with nefarious intent. Although not immediately relevant to the current discussion, here is an example of how readily we share actual, mainly demographic, information about our real selves in online interactions and transactions. In April 2010, the now dissolved retail group *Gamestation* amended its terms and conditions to state "By placing an order via this web site on the first day of the fourth month of the year 2010 Anno Domini, you agree to grant Us a non transferable option to claim, for now and for ever more, your immortal soul". None of the 7500 customers who made an online purchase that day queried this (see http://www.out-law.com/page-10929 for the full story).

The findings from Attrill and Jalil (2011) and Attrill (2012b) were interpreted as indicating that different types of self-information could be selectively and voluntarily called upon to guide self-disclosures and the sharing of personal information depending upon (1) the type of website or application being used and (2) the goal of self-disclosing self-information. One hypothesis that future research could thus address is whether people are more likely to portray the real self when faced with involuntary disclosures to achieve a desired goal. However, on considering this notion further, a psychological tension could be created should a person need to reveal information about their real self when they actually want to represent a more ideal version of self online.

The Communication Privacy Management Theory (CPMT) put forward by Petronio (2002, 2007) considers the way in which people

DOI: 10.1057/9781137483416.0006

deal with the tension of the necessary paradox of needing to share self-information online in order to achieve behavioural or psychological goals, with the need for privacy and not sharing private information. This theory could help explain the differences between voluntary and involuntary self-disclosures online. The tension discussed by Petronio may be similar to that arising from a person's want for holding back information about his/her real self to project a more idealistic view of self online. Although Petronio suggests that individuals' motivation influence the setting of their own privacy rules, five basic principles are suggested to guide their online sharing of personal information:

1   A belief in the ownership of one's private information.
2   Perceived control over the dissemination of personal information to others.
3   Personal boundaries of self-disclosure are monitored by the individual.
4   Assumption of other people accepting one's own defined personal boundaries.
5   Conflict will arise if a boundary is overstepped.

In further work by Petronio and Durham (2008), the model is used to elucidate how people control the revelation of their private information. In terms of involuntarily needing to share aspects of the real self, as long as people feel that they own that information, are in control of who sees it and can delete it at any time, they may be more willing to divulge it. Increasingly, websites are including options to opt out of the sharing of a person's private demographic information to third parties. If a person knows this to be the case, then the desire to achieve a goal of voluntarily sharing carefully constructed self-information may outweigh the need to involuntarily reveal the actual self. This would suggest the need for some level of trust in order to reveal actual self-information in these online situations.

4.6   Trust and privacy concerns

One factor that has not yet been considered as having an effect on how we engage in online impression management and creating the self online is that of trust. The first type of trust that affects self-presentation is one of accepting that an Internet provider has security measures in place to ensure that self-information is safely and securely transmitted. A web-site may however instil trust without being trustworthy. A trustworthy website would be one that follows through on a promise or transaction. A website for online shopping that is associated with a large well-known retailer might for instance be more trustworthy than is a little unknown online shop. A further form of trust, and probably the most important for the current discussion, is that associated with online interpersonal communication. Regardless of how people interact online, they will be sharing some aspect of their self. They put their trust in the recipient of an email, for instance, that s/he will not further distribute that communication, especially if it is personal in content. This type of implicit trust placed in other people will likely shape self-presentation across various forms of online communication, especially of an interpersonal nature.

Consider, for instance, how you build up trust in relationships both online and offline. Offline, you might meet someone in a pub. You may implicitly trust this person until they give you cause not to trust them. Alternatively, you may not trust them at all until they have earned your trust, especially since too much trust can affect our feelings of privacy, emotional well-being and even physical well-being and safety (Yamagishi, 2001). Yamagishi therefore suggests that we engage in a cautious optimal level of trust in the initial stages of a relationship, enough trust to pro-long the interaction but not enough trust so as to be taken advantage of. Offline, people also exist within a wider social circle. As soon as you enter that circle via friends or family, you are likely to receive second or third-hand stories of the individual along with social cues which could enhance or decrease your level of trust in them. Online, you are unlikely to have access to a similar extended network, unless of course you meet on, or are added to a social networking page or use a tool useful for warranting (see Section 3.5). This *trust verification* may thus be more difficult to establish online than offline. This should not, however, be taken to imply that people are more able to create a false personality or misrepresent themselves easier online than offline. There is an array of individual and situational factors outlined in Chapters 3 and 5 that play a role in the likelihood of such misrepresentation. That said, there are now plenty of examples of people creating all sorts of personae online for nefarious intent. One need only watch a few episodes of the MTV series *Catfish* to establish that people often misrepresent themselves online for a whole range of reasons. In this programme, a meeting is promoted between people who have been communicating online for a

DOI: 10.1057/9781137483416.0006

period of time. The catfish is presented as the person who has misrepresented themselves in order to attract another person. This person is presented as the catfish's victim. It is also important to point out that the catfish are not always evil nefarious individuals. Rather, often they may misrepresent themselves online to protect certain fragile aspects of their core self. Upon revelation of even the most positive of reasons for engaging in duplicitous behaviour, however, it is noteworthy that the victim's trust in the catfish is damaged. They are not the person they pretended to be and thereby have often irrevocably abused the victim's trust. Trust is thus a bidirectional tool in online interpersonal relationships: People manipulate their cyberself in order to evoke trust in another person, but at the same time they are trusting that the other person is representing their true self online. A related but distinct factor that also influences online self-presentation, especially by affecting self-disclosure is that of privacy concerns.

Privacy concerns may be linked with trust in many different ways. In order to complete almost any activity online, people need to share some level of personal information. In work that considers both trust and privacy concerns online, Joinson, Reips, Buchanan and Paine-Schofield (2010) point out that many websites across the Internet now store any personal information shared by the user. This could pose a threat to peoples' perceived levels of privacy online, that is, their *privacy concern*. Gibbs, Ellison and Lai (2011, p. 71) describe privacy concerns as "what to disclose, to whom, and how to ensure that others are disclosing honestly in return". These concerns could affect how much information people are willing to share online, but could also play a large role in how they selectively share information in such a way as to be manipulating presentation of the cyberself. A lot of work that considers trust and privacy concerns, especially relating to online self-disclosure tend to treat these as two completely distinct factors, but this may not be the case. Some studies demonstrate that trust mediates the relationship between privacy concerns and self-disclosure (e.g., Malhotra, Kim & Agarwal, 2004; Metzger, 2004). It would thus appear that trust and privacy concerns are somewhat intertwined in enabling people to freely and selectively present themselves online in a goal-directed manner to complete a goal. One way in which this entanglement may be explained is to borrow from a Social Psychological Theory of reward and cost. Based on Social Exchange Theory, Dinev and Hart (2006) suggest a *privacy calculus perspective* of online self-disclosure and self-presentation to draw *trusting beliefs* and

DOI: 10.1057/9781137483416.0006

privacy concerns together with *anticipated benefits* of an online action (see also Section 4.5 on Petronio's (2002, 2007) CPMT). Although the privacy concerns reflect the negative feature of presenting or sharing the self online, the anticipation of a positive outcome (e.g., social acceptance or enjoyment) provides the benefit element to this cost-benefit evaluation. The trusting beliefs reflect the sharer's trust in the communications recipient(s) or partner(s) being perceived as having some form of benefit to the sharer. This cost-benefit consideration to online self-presentation has been demonstrated by Koroleva, Brecht, Goebel and Malinova (2011) when showing that the benefits to be achieved by individuals' posts to a SNS were influenced by privacy awareness factors. It would thus appear that both trust and privacy concerns are very important determinants of how people share self-information online in order to create a cyberself, and whether that cyberself reflects an actual, ideal or ought self.

On reflecting upon the writing of this chapter, a final note is made of pondering whether the involuntary sharing of the self online is a reflection of an ought cyberself. Though there appears to be no empirical consideration of this notion in the available literature, it could well be the case. The ought self is based on who a person believes they should be in a given situation (Higgins, 1987). Involuntary sharing revolves around people needing to create a version of the self online in such a way as to meet others' demands and requirements, regardless of whether those "other" are people or websites. This notion offers a line of consideration that may benefit from future research.

DOI: 10.1057/9781137483416.0006

5
The Social Cognitive Internet and the Cyberself

Abstract: *By far the widest area of impact upon how people construct and maintain their online selves appears to stem from situational and social cognitive features of online interactions. This chapter therefore outlines a number of now classical features of social and social cognitive factors that influence online relationships. In doing so, it also explores a new take on a theory that could be used to understand online impression management from a selective, motivated memory-system model perspective. Social factors that impinge play an interactive role in driving online self-presentation that are considered in this chapter include the moral self, promiscuous befriending and the desire to attain social capital. Before providing concluding comments on the whole text, the chapter focuses on the role of culture in self-presentation and the notion of different Internet arenas being synonymous with different cultures. It therefore also focuses on the very different online cultures of gaming and online support arenas.*

Key words: culture; situational factors; social capital; social cognitive factors; support

Attrill, Alison. *The Manipulation of Online Self-Presentation: Create, Edit, Re-edit and Present.* Basingstoke: Palgrave Macmillan, 2015. DOI: 10.1057/9781137483416.0007.

Although some researchers have focused on understanding the cyberself from a personality perspective, it is difficult to conceive of online interactions being driven by, or resulting solely from, individual characteristics, or indeed the way in which people share self-information online. Offline people act out a variety of *social roles* in their everyday activities, more often than not based upon the situation in which they find themselves. At this particular point in time, you might be playing the role of student, researcher or educator. When you finish work, you may go home and play the role of husband, wife, partner, mother or father. These reflect different aspects of your self that may have arisen from the social norms of the society within which you function. *Social norms* are the rules and regulations of societies. They can derive from a wider societal enforcement of what is socially acceptable, as well as from one's own understanding of how others expect a person to behave in certain situations. Offline, there are many situational cues and factors that influence how a person presents themselves. These can include, but are not limited to, the type of situation in which a person finds themselves, the people with whom they are interacting or aspects of the surroundings over which no one has control. Currently, there appears to be no single theory that enables predictions of how different situations influence the way in which people express their personality and therewith their self (Ten Berge & De Raad, 1999). That said, Clifton's (2014) social network analysis approach (see Section 3.1) did consider the role of situational factors among a social network of 31 individuals. Participants were asked to consider their own personality in relation to each of 30 members of their own social network. While Clifton observed that people might change expressions of different aspects of their personalities depending upon the relationship in which they are currently interacting, there remains no definitive theory that situational factors determine that expression of the self. On the Internet, situational factors are largely determined by the different types of Internet arenas available for interaction. These are not, however, merely observed. There is some level of interpretation prior and during interaction that may be cognitively determined in order to continuously edit and present the cyberself. The following section gives a brief overview of a theory which suggests online self-presentation to reflect a selective goal-directed process by taking these interpretations into consideration. It offers a blended approach that adds a cognitive component to the goal-directed approach outlined thus far in understanding online self-portrayals. Subsequently, consideration will be given to various

DOI: 10.1057/9781137483416.0007

factors which substantiate the proposal of a social cognitive approach to understanding online self-presentation.

5.1   Social cognitive factors

One of the underlying premises of purist social psychology is that all human behaviour is a product of the environment in which people are raised and exist. From a more recent social cognitive perspective, humans are not mere bystanders who soak up everything that is happening around them like a sponge. Rather, they engage in cognitive processing to perceive, interpret and respond to situational factors and events. Upon perceiving that a person is about to engage in a certain behaviour, for instance, you might retrieve from memory similar experiences of what happened when you engaged in the same or a similar behaviour. This autobiographical memory will then guide how you interpret the person's intended action and how you respond should s/he either avoid or continue with the action. People are bound not only by situational factors, but also by how they have constructed their self cognitively in relation to previous events and people in their lives. Social factors, the environment and cognitive process thus interact to create and maintain an understanding of one's own self-concept and self-identity, processes which also influence how other people, items, objects and events are perceived and interpreted.

This social cognitive line of reasoning was brought about by consideration of the idea that people do not consistently display the same self across different Internet arenas. Attrill (2012b) found, for example, that there were differences in the types and levels of self-information reportedly shared on different types of Internet website. Following on from work carried out by Attrill and Jalil (2011) in which it was shown that people selectively share different types of self-information online, Attrill (2012b) interpreted the observed selective categorical sharing reported by participants according to a *social cognitive memory system model* (Conway & Pleydell-Pearce, 2000) which suggests that people selectively retrieve self-information in a goal-directed manner. According to the *self-memory-system model* (SMS), humans have a hierarchical categorical storage of all information relating to the self. Any information that they encounter is stored into this system based upon certain characteristics of the event, person, object or item that they are recording. For

DOI: 10.1057/9781137483416.0007

instance, information pertaining to one's relationship status might be encoded into the category of information about one's marriage; information about one's dog would be encoded into a category of the self as a dog owner. The hierarchy of self-referent information is stored within an autobiographical knowledge base over which one has selective and conscious control. The *lifetime periods* level of information contains the most basic self-information, such as one's interests, and feeds into a *general events* level of self-information. The general events level is slightly more detailed and contains more specific information about certain occurrences in one's life. The highest level of self-information is that of *event-specific knowledge*, which contains the most intimate feelings, beliefs and knowledge about oneself. There is a flow of information from the superficial lifetime periods to general events and subsequently to the most personal and detailed information of the event specific knowledge categories of self-information. Attrill (2012b) and Attrill and Jalil (2011) likened this progression of self-information storage to the gradual sharing and revealing of self-information characteristic of Altman and Taylor's (1973) Social Penetration Theory (SPT), especially in terms of the voluntary revelation of information about the self to other people. Across two studies they used an adaptation of Magno's (2009) self-disclosure scale to measure revelations of information about *personal matters, interests, intimate feelings, beliefs* and *relationships*. Although Attrill and Jalil (2011) proposed the gradual and progressive voluntary self-disclosure of self-information that could be mapped onto the SMS model, Attrill (2012b) demonstrated differences in the categories of information revealed across different types of Internet arena in a way that reflected different categories of self-information that may be stored at different levels of the self-memory system model. At the time, these considerations were of the first to outline how online self-disclosure might be considered from a social cognitive model perspective to understanding the sharing of self-information online. As pointed out by Nguyen, Bin and Campbell (2012), there had thus far been no single theory that could account for observations of different types and amounts of self-information being shared online. Moreover, these two studies were important in demonstrating that people are far more selective in how they present their self-information and how much of the self they reveal online than had hitherto been suggested. This proposal is substantiated by observations of a number of factors that impinge upon a person's selective online self-portrayal, such as social norms,

DOI: 10.1057/9781137483416.0007

situational and cultural factors, and the types of relationships sought out, or played out, online.

5.2   Social norms and situational factors

On the Internet, and in particular on social networking sites (SNSs), we are able to create and manipulate presentation of our self to others (Ellison, Heino & Gibbs, 2006; Utz, 2010). Maghrabi, Oakley & Nemati (2014) suggest that SNSs carry a freedom of self-representation that promotes the exhibition of diverse aspects of an individual's identity. They go on to suggest that individuals may continuously reconstruct their cyberself on SNSs to gain and maintain social bonds. Particularly if using asynchronous communication, individuals have the advantage of controlling and manipulating their self-presentation online. However, though they are able to create any invention of their cyberself that they wish to, repeated and constant editing or recreation of the self could lead to a sense of inconsistency in the self both to the self and others. Over-monitoring and editing of self-content could thus affect the relationships that one has online (Ellison et al., 2006). As pointed out by Maghrabi et al. (2014), the benefits derived from the online relationships could also be negatively impacted through over-monitoring (Lin, 2002; Portes, 1998).

Situational factors are reflected online in the different types of Internet arena that people use, regardless of whether they are intentionally visiting any given website with the intention of fostering impression management. It is more likely that people change their cyberself depending upon the type of website being frequented. An individual might use different profile pictures and information about the self on a dating website compared to a SNS. Often, the social norms associated with a particular website might guide the type of cyberself presented. For example, there are now a number of academic-related research hubs on the Internet, such as ResearchGate (http://www.researchgate.net/). These are websites intended for the portrayal of the professional self, including academic qualifications, research interests and recent publications. We would not expect the same information to be portrayed on these websites as might be the case on a SNS. Although individual and social identities offline are influenced by social and cultural norms, it may thus be the case that expressions of one's cyberself are becoming increasingly influenced by

DOI: 10.1057/9781137483416.0007

a new set of online social norms. People already talk of *email etiquette* as if we have always understood the implicit rules of email engagement. Violations of such etiquette might at first glance carry little consequence, but this is unlikely the case, but they could be hugely detrimental to both online and offline relationships. Given that human relationships are one of the underlying social foundations of an ever-evolving Internet, attention now turns to this particular social feature of the Internet.

5.3 Online relationships

It is not really surprising that the Internet evolved very quickly as a means of communicating and forging social bonds, regardless of communicators' geographical locations. In order to do so, however, self-information needs to be shared in a way that entices people to engage with one another. There are very good outlines available of how humans have evolved methods of creating and maintaining relationships over the years via emerging technologies, from Standage's (1998) *Victorian Telegraph* to Whitty and Carr's (2006) comparison of *courtly love* to *cyberflirting*. From the moment that mankind learned to communicate via pictures and written text, people have learned ways of sharing aspects of self with the aim of creating relationships and a sense of belonging. Indeed, returning to Goffman's (1959) Theory of Self-Presentation (see Section 2.1), there has long since been a suggestion that humans will selectively manage impressions of themselves to gain social liking and acceptance. Myddleton and Attrill (2015) provide a full overview of various types of relationships such as *working* and *familial ties* in online behaviour, but for the purposes of this text, the two main types of *romantic* and *platonic* relationships will be focused upon in relation to satisfying the needs of liking, acceptance and belonging online. Nearly all types of online relationship thrive on some level of self-presentation and a very carefully manipulated and controlled impression management. Whereas many people who seek out romantic relationships online may want to transfer them offline at some stage, platonic relationships, or *friendships* as they are more commonly known, may exist between people who are merely acquainted and will never meet offline.

Platonic relationships may revolve around a completely different set of norms for self-presentation and management online to romantic relationships. Both can however exist entirely in the cybersphere without

DOI: 10.1057/9781137483416.0007

any communications partners ever finding out who they are actually interacting with. This can be achieved through pictorial representations (e.g., avatars) or through nick-names used to hide one's true identity. It is interesting to note that much early work which examined online relationship formation discusses, for example, how only 7.9% of 60.7% relationships reportedly formed in online newsgroups were romantically intended (Parks & Floyd, 1986), or that of 93.6% of relationships formed in *multi-object orientation arenas* (MOOs) 40.6% were aimed at building close friendships, while only 36.3% were romantically intended (Parks & Roberts, 1998). Online friendships may therefore be just as important to people as are their offline friendships, possibly serving similar functions. We will return later to considering whether platonic online interactions can serve the function of socialising not met in an offline world for some individuals, but for now, it is important to illustrate that there can be positive effects of building friendships online.

Valkenburg and Peter (2007) demonstrated that online friendships can have a positive effect on one's offline self. They found that Dutch teenagers reported significant positive effects of online communications on their overall sense of well-being, especially if the communication took place via private instant messaging rather than using more public exchanges. The effect was also reduced if exchanges were between strangers, supporting the idea that in order to reveal the real self to another online, communication likely needs to ensue in a gradual progressive manner. Although this work is only 7–8 years old, there have been vast changes to online computer-mediated communication (CMC) since 2007, with developments in both synchronous and asynchronous communication tools, from webcams to chat apps, as well as increases in the types of website used on the Internet. It is now far more acceptable, for example, to build relationships via dating websites. SNSs have also possibly permanently changed the way in which humans communicate and interact. All of these changes bring with them the need to distinguish how humans achieve both romantic and non-romantic relationships online, and how much of their core or true self, if any, they use in doing so. It is likely that which self is presented very much depends upon the use of the Internet as a tool to achieve the gratification of the type of relationship sought. In line with Altman and Taylor's (1973) SPT, it might be the case that if a romantic relationship is sought, the person may be more likely to initially portray a desired or ideal self, with the real self emerging over time as trust is established between the communicators.

DOI: 10.1057/9781137483416.0007

The other side of this self-presentation coin is that the person to whom one depicts one's true or ideal self may create an idealised version of that individual, possibly to the extent that such a relationship begins to take precedence over their offline social interactions. Such relationships can also become very intense, whether based on the real, ideal or ought self, sometimes even to the point of becoming hyperpersonal (Walther, 1996). That said, if the goal of online interactions is to move them to one's offline world, then conveying the real self from the outset is probably the most sensible tactic, as evidenced in McKenna, Green & Gleason (2002) study which demonstrated that among online newsgroups when people conveyed their true self, they were more likely to develop strong online relationships that could be successfully transferred offline. On thinking about all of these social factors that influence the portrayal of the cyber-self, one feature of online behaviour that springs to mind is the level of deceit or deception involved in portraying even a slightly exaggerated core self to others online. Surely, there is a sense of responsibility and some level of one's own morality involved in these portrayals, even if they are not intended as manipulated or controlled impression management exploits.

5.4 The moral self

One way that the cyberself might have an impact on one's offline self is through an individual's appraisals and moral evaluations of people and situations. *Morals* are messages about behaviour that are often conveyed through tales and stories. These are then applied by individuals when they engage in *moral reasoning*. In an uncertain situation which requires a decision between right and wrong, humans engage in a process of reasoning to determine which course of action to take, guided by their own morals. As they are acquired throughout life, morals could be conceived of as a learned form of cognitive appraisal and reasoning which help shape one's own self-construct. One's malleable self-identity could thus be influenced by any moral content to which one is exposed in a way that shapes one's core self.

If we cast our minds back just 30–40 years, when mass media comprised mainly of printed material, the television and film industries, boundaries of acceptability were a lot higher than they appear to be nowadays. Although television programmes in the 1970s may have thrived

DOI: 10.1057/9781137483416.0007

on double entendre, rarely were scenes of sex and intimacy shown, and certainly not during the afternoon or early evening hours. Nowadays, people have instant access to almost any desired content via the Internet. This content may not always be legal, but it is there. It is readily available and it is shaping how people conceptualise and construct their core selves. On considering exactly this feature of the Internet, Seibt and Nørskov (2012, p. 286) ask whether we as a people are "losing our sense of self in the multiplication of our 'identities' or self-presentations on the internet, and if so, are we losing the very ground of moral agency?" This is an interesting, yet rarely researched aspect of the cyberself. Seibt and Nørskov consider the ethical aspects of disembodiment and anonymity on the Internet and how the absence of physical contact could contribute to changing moral standards. They proposed the *Model of Personal Identity*, according to which humans use evaluative judgements and commitments to describe both their own and others' experiences. Outlining first, second and third person perspectives that come together to provide people with an evaluative judgement of a situation, they propose that individuals experience multiple self-presentations online, each of which may be different, but yet can be somehow reconciled to enable the person to function in a moral manner. Although this may well be the case, Turkle (1995) might have very well interpreted these multiple selves as an individual exploring the self online. The model is fairly new and has not yet undergone rigorous testing. In order to demonstrate the multiplication of identities proposed by Seibt and Nørskov, research would need to consider not only the wide and varied types of Internet sites that a person may use online, but also other factors that play a role in shaping their online self-presentations, such as how they change the cyberself depending upon the possibly varied audience receiving that information.

5.5   The multiple audience problem

How people present themselves to others online is also influenced by other people. Take for instance SNSs such as Facebook. A profile page is created on Facebook that allows other people to have input via status updates. While the page owner might be able to control who sees their posts and who is allowed to post to their page, they nonetheless offer people the opportunity to have input into how they are represented

DOI: 10.1057/9781137483416.0007

on that page as well as on others' pages. If they are striving to present themselves in a controlled manner, one that projects their best possible self, input from others could be damaging. There is some evidence to suggest that the input provided by other people on one's page may not be construed, managed or manipulated, thus possibly reflecting more of the poster's accurate or real self rather than the ideal they are editing and promoting (e.g., Walther, Van Der Heide, Hamel & Schulman, 2009; Walther, Van Der Heide, Kim, Westerman & Tong, 2008) (see Section 2.5 for an outline of the related Warranting Theory). The *multiple audience problem* refers to exactly this inability to manage multiple others' expectations about one's behaviour (Leary, 1995). On Facebook, a person may be friends with work colleagues, school friends, their parents and partner, as well as having acquaintances who they have never met offline. The selective recipient option is often a useful tool in selecting who can interact with and see one's Facebook page, as is the opportunity to review any posts by others prior to them appearing on one's page. However, some posts will need to be considered in relation to how all of these diverse others expect the individual to behave. Hogan (2010) suggests that the multiple audience problem is circumvented by carefully selecting and sharing information acceptable to all friends and acquaintances. This sort of behaviour further emphasises the notion that people use the Internet to meet certain behavioural goals. The goal here being a selective self-presentation and manipulation dependent upon whom one wishes to see online content. Reflecting a selective process of self-presentation, it also raises the question as to whether this sharing then reflects a true representation of the self or a carefully constructed cyberself. This is a question maybe partly answered in how selective people are in their befriending behaviours online.

5.6   The promiscuous befriender and distant self

One aspect of online behaviour that is difficult to replicate offline is that of *promiscuous friending*. Online, people often lower their boundaries of sharing information with others with the intention of making friends online (e.g., Rui & Stefanone, 2013). Promiscuous friending occurs when people simply add others to their friends list on a SNS to inflate their audience size. This may occur with the aim of gaining attention from more people, or it might be a strategy used to gain popularity from others. However, there is a trade-off to be paid in engaging in promiscuous friending: The more people added to a given group, the wider the opportunity for others to reveal one's real rather than desired self online. Consequently, the poster would need to engage in far more protective self-presentation in order to avert and amend or clarify any posts that could potentially harm the ideal self image that they are striving to portray (Arkin, 1981). One such protective strategy may lie in distancing behaviours.

From a psychological perspective, distance can be conceived of in a number of ways, including *physical distance* (actual tangible distance between people), *emotional distance* (the discrepancy in how people feel about a given situation) and *temporal distance* (differences in time). Along with the synchronicity of a chosen mode of online communication, distance can affect how people present their cyberself. There are reports that physical distance can exaggerate a person's sense of romantic intensity, especially if fewer resources are required to sustain an online relationship (e.g., Ben-Ze'ev, 2005). Ortony, Clore & Collings (1988) suggest that any form of distance is nothing other than a psychological construct rather than a geographical feature. If this is the case, people should expect distance to play no role in online self-presentations. Of importance should be the interpretation of others' online self-presentations. This is not the case. In fact, temporal distance has been shown to intensify emotions (McIntosh & Martin, 1992), possibly due to increased levels of rumination. Rumination could be of either a positive or negative nature, especially since online relationships thrive on interpreting written communications. Moreover, while considering written exchanges enables people to think about others' online presentations from different angles, it could also lead to focusing on certain aspects of the communication or characteristics of the communicator which, in turn, could lead to a distorted view of the communicator, possibly a view of admiration or creating one's own idealised view of the communications partner (e.g., McIntosh & Martin, 1992). If a relationship plays out entirely online, this would likely be of little consequence unless the relationship takes on a hyperpersonal nature or interferes with the maintenance of offline relationships. When online communications are used to enhance or maintain existing relationships, however, one would hope that a more honest portrayal of the offline self would ensue, since verification of aspects of the cyberself would be more easily achieved offline than online.

DOI: 10.1057/9781137483416.0007

5.7   Social capital

Thus far the self has been considered somewhat as a single entity, a construct from within that emerges from our learning and social experiences with the external world. As John Donne (1572–1631) once wrote "No man is an island, entire of itself, every man is a piece of the continent, a part of the main ..." in his poem *For Whom The Bell Tolls* (*No Man Is An Island*). People rarely exist alone. They thrive from interacting with others, which essentially underlies the notion of this book of people creating cyberselves to achieve human interaction. Therefore, consideration needs to be given to the reasons why humans as social beings seek benefits from their online self-portrayals. The variety of interactions that people experience in life, both online and offline can create a rich tapestry of influences on one's self-identity and self-presentation. Across different situations people might express different aspects of their self, some aimed at creating long-lasting intense bonds with other people and some interactions with others who are of absolutely no consequence or importance. Online, people create *weak* and *strong bonds* with others, only some of which will strongly influence how they present the cyberself. The creation and presentation of self can be monitored and manipulated to enhance or weaken these bonds, both offline and online, in a way that creates interactions and social bonds that provide people with *social capital* (e.g., Lin, 2002; Portes, 1998). Social capital refers to the resources created through social interactions and relationships. These can be tangible resources such as housing or money, or psychological resources such as emotional support. The social capital might not exist in a direct one-to-one relationship, but might be an artefact of an extended social network. As suggested by Granovetter (1982), the way that this social capital is used can create two types of relationship:

Bonding relationships: strong ties; often found in close emotional relationships, usually with family and close friends
Bridging relationships: weak ties; found in larger social networks, often among a larger group of friends, or those who have similar interests/goals

In turn, which type of ties are created online can positively or negatively affect social relationships by creating two different types of social capital, *productive social capital* (interactions that reap positive social benefits) and *perverse social capital* (interactions that result in negative social benefits).

DOI: 10.1057/9781137483416.0007

How individuals monitor and present the self on different websites will influence the resulting types of relationship and social capital. In other words, what people put in, in terms of self-presentation and impression management, influences what they take from these online relationships. Although some individuals might actively self-monitor their online self-presentation with the intent of increasing their social capital, others might inadvertently create perverse social capital (see e.g., Claridge, 2004).

One advantage of the Internet is that it could enable people to connect with others and build social capital in a way in which they otherwise would not be able to do. If, for instance, someone is mobility impaired and cannot leave the house, then the Internet might provide their only form of social interaction. If this is used as a social lifeline, then it stands to reason that the user would want to represent him/her in the best possible light with the intention of maximising productive social capital. SNSs offer a unique way to achieve this. Let us consider for example, if the mobility impaired person wants to explore new social connections online before transferring these connections to their offline world. They might be testing out acceptance of a version of their self that they do not feel comfortable presenting offline, possibly for fear of social rejection (e.g., Pennebaker, 1989). The online portrayal might empower the individual or provide them with an otherwise absent sense of control over their social existence. That is not to say that people who seek online social capital might be so inconsistent in their self-presentations that they may inadvertently create perverse social capital (e.g., Utz, 2010).

On considering the interaction of attempting to attain productive social capital and facets of self-presentation on SNSs, Maghrabi et al. (2014) point out that control and manipulation of one's SNS profile to promote interaction with a select sub-category of befriended others may constrain or reduce opportunities to create social bonds with other people. Moreover, as noted by Adler and Kwon (2002), in their consideration of groups such as terrorist organisations and self-harm groups, immersing oneself into a certain type of group to foster strong bonds within that group at the cost of strengthening bonds with other people could result in disastrous offline consequences. Thus, manipulating self-presentation in a craving for strong but negative social capital could achieve exactly the opposite, weak but positive offline ties become even looser. Ellison et al. (2006) also point out that creating some level of bonding social capital in SNSs is essential to the attainment of support in

DOI: 10.1057/9781137483416.0007

one's offline world. It may however be the case that online relationships serve to enhance social capital by compensating online for relationships not experienced offline.

The *social compensation hypothesis* (SCH) suggests that people engage in online behaviours to achieve something that they are lacking or missing in their offline lives (Davis & Kraus, 1989), whereas the *social enhancement hypothesis* (SEH) proposed that peoples' online behaviour is an extension of their offline self (Valkenburg, Schouten &Peter, 2005). Thus, according to the SEH an extravert engages in highly sociable behaviours both online and offline, whereas the SCH suggests that an introvert or shy person may seek out relationships online that s/he does not have offline. Support for the SEH comes from Hampton, Goulet, Rainie & Purcell (2011) who found that SNS users experienced close ties to their offline network, suggesting that their online activities served to enhance their offline networks. Papacharissi and Mendelson (2011) demonstrated that people who are active offline are most likely to use SNSs to create ties with others online. As yet, there exists work to support both the SCH and SEH, leading to the suggestion that different people may use the Internet in a goal-directed manner for different purposes. Whereas some may use it to enhance their social relationships, others might seek social compensation online. These two concepts have been thus far treated as distinct entities with no overlap or consideration that the same person might engage in different types of behaviours on different types of websites in order to create both social compensation for those facets of their offline lives that are missing, but social enhancement for those features that are considered positive in their offline world. Of note is also the observation that social capital is not purely driven by the individual but is also a facet of the society or culture in which that person exists. The social norms and situational influences that play a role in any social interaction or behaviour are often grounded in the culture in which they are being carried out. Online behaviour is no different in this instance to offline behaviour, with culture influencing how people portray their cyberself.

5.8   Offline and online cultures

Culture is "a complex frame of reference that consists of patterns of traditions, beliefs, values, norms, and meanings that are shared in varying

DOI: 10.1057/9781137483416.0007

degrees by interacting members of a community" (Ting-Toomey, 1999, p.10). One of the most commonly used models of culture is that proposed by Hofstede (1980), according to which, culture is a concept bound with many facets of human behaviour, including national and self-identity. Hofstede proposed four dimensions along which culture can be observed *Individualism/collectivism, Power distance, Uncertainty* and *Masculinity*. The dimension that has been most used in terms of understanding cultural impacts on online behaviour is that of individualism and collectivism. Collectivist cultures are characterised by wanting what is best for the collective, for the group, rather than providing focus and attention to the individual as is the case in individualist cultures. Rosen, Stefanone and Lackaff (2010) observed evidence for this cultural dimension affecting the sharing of photographs on SNSs, whereby posters shared photos in individualistic cultures in order to garner attention, while those in a collectivist culture shared pictures with a focus on group harmony. Further cultural differences in online presentation were observed by Rui and Stefanone (2013). They asked participants from the USA and Singapore how many friends they had on a SNS. Americans more frequently posted text-based wall posts and Singaporeans posted more photos.

Following on the distinction between collectivist and independent cultures, Markus and Kitayama (1991) suggested that people create a self according to either independent or interdependent self-construals. Whereas *independent self-construals* refers to focus on internal, private aspects of self as distinct from the environment and social contexts, *interdependent self-construals* focus on external, public aspects of self intertwined with the environment and social contexts. Independent individuals are thus characteristic of individualistic cultures, and interdependent individuals of collectivist cultures.

Triandis (1994) also put forward a distinction between *idiocentric* and *allocentric* individuals, whereby idiocentrics are akin to those people who create independent self-construals and allocentrics are those whose identities are based on interdependent self-construals. Both of these conceptualisations of self are very much directed and constructed through the environment in which an individual exists. However, aspects of the self remain fluid and malleable and either the idiocentric (independent) or the allocentric (interdependent) self can become dominant to guide interactions depending upon the situation in which one finds oneself. Although there is a large offline cultural influence on this saliency, of interest here is whether this salience occurs online, and if so, whether

DOI: 10.1057/9781137483416.0007

people present and manage either their idiocentric or allocentric self depending upon the online environment within which they are presenting the self. There is some work by Chen and Markus (2012) which had 463 American Psychology students complete a questionnaire about their online disclosures. One of their key findings was that participants low on idiocentrism shared the least honest self-information online, but they were more likely to share information that they considered to be relevant to the intended reader or audience. This suggests that people are selectively self-presenting in a manner which addresses the multiple audience problem. In other words, they are using the Internet in a goal-directed manner that is influenced by their cultural identity. If culture influences one's identity and different types of Internet website could be considered as different environments akin to offline cultures because they have certain norms and societal influences associated with them, then it might be the case that the choice of Internet arena could also influence one's online self-presentation. On considering the role of different Internet arenas, however, it may emerge that maybe research should move away from thinking about the different influence of certain factors in online compared to offline behaviours, to considering different types of Internet website as online cultures in their own right. Rather than thinking of cultures online and offline, research may benefit from considering diverse Internet arenas as different types of online culture.

5.8.1   Online cultures and diverse Internet arenas

A lot of early research on online behaviour focused on comparisons of online to offline activities. In those early days this may have been feasible, when there were very few ways of communicating online, with most CMC occurring via email or other forms of asynchronous exchanges. Nowadays, the Internet is awash with many different modes of communication, from the text-based asynchronous and personal instant messaging or email to the self-broadcasting of YouTube and other social media. Finding equivalents to compare to in the offline world becomes rather difficult. Consider the joyous event of a wedding. Many years ago, the happy couple would have been pleased to have some black and white photos of the event. A few years later, a couple may have had colour photos, prior to it becoming popular to film the event in the latter half of the 20th century. The video cassette of the wedding may have eventually found its way to the back of the cupboard, being dug out for viewing on special occasions. It is extremely unlikely that it would have been shown

DOI: 10.1057/9781137483416.0007

to more than the closest family and friends of the couple. What is the modern equivalent? People have always, and will always, want to share happy occasions with other people. Regardless of the era and mode of sharing, the self-identity of the sharer is influenced by the response from those with whom the events are shared. Nowadays, social media plays a large role in both happy and sad life events that shape human beings' identities. If celebrating a wedding, then the couple may want people on social media to like their photos of the occasion. In doing so, they are reaffirming the couple's sense of positive identity in this association to their wedded other. If sharing a sad event such as the loss of a significant person in one's life, then peoples' comments on social media can be reassuring and help create a feeling of being warranted in one's grief. This affirmation of the positive and warranting of the negative on such a grandiose scale has no equivalent in the offline world. It may be likened to larger societal or cultural events that cause happiness or grief for the masses but these are unlikely driven by an individual expressing those emotions. That said, it has become somewhat commonplace for people to share the most private moments of their life, possibly with the goal of seeking affirmation, positive reinforcement and a sense of belonging. It appears that celebrities are evermore pushing the boundaries of seeking such approval and acceptance via social media. You may have recently witnessed the birth of Robbie Williams' second child as he continuously Tweeted pictures and videos of himself and wife throughout the labour. Was this in bad taste? Was it a step too far in the pursuit of self-aggrandizement of his accomplishments and positive reinforcement of his achievements as his singing and dancing took precedence in the video clips over his wife's labour pains? Or, was it simply a further demonstration of how online activities for one person can influence the offline masses and help create a new online social norm of behaviour? In an attempt to understand Robbie Williams' editing and broadcasting of his self in this instance, there is simply no offline equivalent. Hopefully, this example illustrates the near impossibility of comparing online like with offline like, but if not, think of online gaming. The online gamer can communicate and compete with anyone and everyone worldwide, interacting with cultures s/he has possibly never heard of. Comparing this to the influence of offline sports on the self is just not feasible. It thus appears far more conducive to consider the Internet as a homogenous landscape that, while having similarities with some offline social situations and interactions, and cultural impact is nonetheless an entity in

DOI: 10.1057/9781137483416.0007

its own right. To illustrate this further, attention is given to the unique entities that are online gaming and virtual environments.

5.9 Virtual worlds and online gaming

As already mentioned in Section 2.2.2, some people seek an experience of flow when playing with others via interactive games. Interactive games are now played via many different technological devices, from game-specific consoles, such as different versions of the Playstation or Xbox, to gaming apps on mobile phones and tablets, to whiling away a work day playing Bejeweled Blitz or Candy Crush on Facebook. The lure of being able to abandon one's daily woes and temporarily lose oneself in a game of choice is now present for many in most aspects of daily life. Where once gamers might have been considered to be geeks or nerds, adolescent boys who locked themselves in their bedrooms to shoot zombies and combat the world, gamers come from all walks of socio-economic background, from all tiers of life. The gaming industry now uses psychological input to develop target-specific games, from bingo for housewives to gambling for the football enthusiast. From free to the massively expensive, there is now a game for every member of society somewhere in the cybersphere. Unlike other forms of online arenas, games might serve a completely different goal to the self. Rather than using this medium to create and manage others' impressions of the self, gaming could be a tool for reaffirming one's perceptions of self.

According to Goffman's (1959) theory of self-presentation (see Section 2.1), people use visual and textual stimuli to express themselves. To enter any form of online gaming, the gamer needs to create a self via a user-name and possibly an avatar. In doing so, s/he may already be manipulating their self-presentation. It is rare that a gamer would use their own name, demographic information and credentials other than as required for the creation of an account, especially if this could be misappropriated for nefarious actions by others. When creating a username, the gamer may over-emphasise certain characteristics if they are particularly pertinent to success in a chosen game, with choice of representation having been shown to be linked to the role that they are playing and the message which they wish to convey (Vasalou, Joinson, Bänziger, Goldie & Pitt, 2008). This raises the question as to whether people retain the same identity regardless of which game they are playing or whether their

DOI: 10.1057/9781137483416.0007

gaming self is so malleable that it can frequently change. Following on from this would be the question as to how big the gap might be between gamers' actual and ideal selves, and whether any psychological effects of such a discrepancy remain purely online or are transferred offline. Consideration could also be given to how people differentially use pictorial and text stimuli to create these different selves in online gaming.

There is a rapidly growing literature that addresses these and further questions around individual identity and online gaming. Evans (2012) provides an excellent overview of work in this area and outlines research which suggests a range of motives for the creation of avatars online, including the creation of a completely different cyberself to the offline self (e.g., Veerapen, 2011), a cyberself that is possible so independent of the offline self that it behaves in a completely different and unforeseen manner (Evans, 2012; Taylor, 2002). There are many gaming realms which we could consider as useful for creating different versions of the self, from the early days of the text-based worlds of MUDs (Multi-user Dungeons) to the more sophisticated realistic avatars that games now use. On MUDs, people were able to create and play out the role of a completely fictitious character, a self that was as compatible or distinct to the actual self as a player desired (e.g., Turkle, 1995). These types of game still exist, with large numbers of people using them daily, but gaming has come a long way since these early MUDs. Therefore, the focus of consideration in the remainder of this section will be on how people use visual and text-based representations of themselves in online gaming.

5.10   Avatars

Some work has considered Higgins' (1987) Self-Discrepancy Theory (SDT) using avatars. Having its origins in the Hinduism descent of a deity or supreme being to Earth, the word *Avatar* in western society is now most commonly associated with a digital representation of the self in a virtual world (VW). Castronova (2005, p. 22) defines *virtual worlds* as "any computer-generated physical space, represented in three dimensions, that can be experienced by many people at once". Using synchronous interaction, virtual worlds or *virtual environments* (VE) are not merely for gaming, but are often used to create online communities based on accepted norms of social structures (e.g., Bainbridge, 2010; Boellstorff, 2008). One example of such a VW is *SecondLife*

DOI: 10.1057/9781137483416.0007

(http://secondlife.com/?sourceid=0313-YahooSEM-Branded_Second-Life-General) which carries the tag line "Your world. Your imagination. The largest-ever 4D virtual world created entirely by its users." When delivering my undergraduate sessions on Cyberpsychology, I often ask students (averaging in age around 19–20 years) if they still use Second Life. They mostly stare at me blankly having never heard of it. Nonetheless, the website seems to thrive on individuals creating an entire online existence in this VW. There are tales of people meeting on Second Life, marrying online and then turning their entire offline existence into turmoil to extend this fantasy life to their offline worlds (see e.g., http://edition.cnn.com/2008/LIVING/12/12/second.life.relationship.irpt/). Although Agger (2004) suggests that creating a cyberself in a VE such as Second Life can provide the connection and sense of belonging that humans crave, it needs to be considered that people may often blur their sense of real and ideal or pretend selves when using these arenas. How real these environments are to the individual will largely depend on their own perceptions of the Internet as real and their online self as an extension of their offline self, or a complete fabrication of a self they would like to be. It may be the use of an avatar that actually fosters this self-creation in VWs.

Avatars enable individuals to act out their different selves online, sometimes playing with their online physical appearance and acting out behaviour (Bailenson & Beall, 2006) in a way which influences the offline self in factors such as self-confidence (Yee & Bailenson, 2007). Yee and Bailenson (2007) found that avatar appearance could affect individual behaviours in a VE based on stereotypes of offline behaviour in a study in which attractive avatars not only walked closer to partnered avatars but also shared more personal information with them than did unattractive avatars. Thus, regardless of who a person may be offline, using a disguise in the form of an avatar online might enable the exploration of their ideal self relating to both societal and personal norms or standards. This role-playing has been shown to enable people to use VEs to explore, edit and recreate themselves, and to subsequently transfer their experiences to the offline world (e.g., Evans, 2012). There may be factors that influence the choice of VE avatar to depict the virtual self. Some evidence suggests that men choose an avatar that is consistent with the goals of the game they are playing, but which simultaneously differs from their actual or real self. Dunn and Guadagno, (2012) assessed self-avatar discrepancies using the Big Five personality

DOI: 10.1057/9781137483416.0007

factors, gender and self-esteem. They found that both men and women selected avatars nearer a public ideal self than their actual selves, especially if they scored highly on the factor of agreeableness. This suggests that people choose avatars that they think reflect a socially acceptable self. They further reported that highly neurotic females were most likely to create attractive avatars, which is in line with the notion that people portray a cyberself that they believe will help them achieve a sense of acceptance, liking or belonging.

Evans (2012) uses Symbolic Interaction Theory and Activity Theory to consider discrepancies between online and offline selves in VEs. According to symbolic interaction theory (James, 1890; Cooley, 1902; Mead, 1956), the self consists of various characters based on the social roles that are played out in daily lives and the different people with whom people interact. This self can react and change to different situations and interactions, responding to one's internal and external worlds. Activity theory (Nardi, 1996) suggests that all of a person's activities are based on the individual carrying out the activity, an objective (or goal) to be completed and the motivations towards carrying out the activity and the actual behavioural execution to attain that goal. In other words, all behaviours, according to activity theory, are goal-directed and constructed through momentary interactions of the self and the environment or context within which a person is acting. Both of these theories suggest that the self is constructed through every day interactions. Evans (2012) argues that the physicality of these interactions can be recreated in VEs, where people who wish to experience social interaction will create ways and means of communicating with the tools that are available rather than using the traditional cues and tools of human interaction. In their most basic and simplest forms, these theories are thus in line with Walther's (1996) notion of compensating online for the absence of any social cues that exist in similar interactions offline, and the suggestion throughout this book that people use the Internet to gratify basic needs and desires in line with the Uses and Gratifications Theory.

The goal, especially in online gaming or a virtual world might, however, simply be one of escapism. If a person is using a VE to compensate their offline social world, for example, a world in which they are not very happy or in which they do not feel accepted, wanted, liked or a part of, they might want their VE self to be as far removed from this reality as possible. From interviews with 40 Second Life users, Evans (2012) provides support for this idea. Participants felt that this VE offered a realm for new interactions with people they would otherwise not encounter or spend significant amounts of time with offline. Of note is that the interviewees felt that they experienced intense emotional experiences in Second Life and that they perceived these to be real and valid interactions even though they perceived their Second Life avatars to represent completely distinct online selves to their offline selves. Evans reports almost a third-party evaluation of these avatar interactions as if the players were looking in upon their own behaviour in a way that enabled them to reflect thereupon and consider the relevance of those interactions to their offline selves (see also Liao, 2011; Taylor, 2002).

Although avatars offer a novel way to experience the self online, one wonders whether this self-creation via an alternative medium is such a new phenomenon. People have always striven to represent themselves through different media, from the written text to film and television as a form of escapism from reality (e.g., Zillman, 1982). After all, what are actors if not creators of various different versions of a self? What avatars do however offer is the possibility to connect socially and emotionally with others, to experience and explore aspects of the self that, for whatever reason, may not be possible, acceptable or even permissible in one's offline culture and/or social environment. Virtual environments could thus play a vital role in helping individuals maintain their offline psychological well-being by allowing them to present their chosen self online. Maybe the way forward is therefore not to consider whether people create distinct or similar cyberselves to their offline selves in VEs, but to consider how the similarities and differences between these two can be used to the advantage of psychological development and well-being, and how they can aid the self-awareness, reflection and recreation of the selves that use them.

5.11   Blogging

Avatars and VE representations of self may serve a very different role to the individual than do other types of online self-expression. Attention therefore now turns to considering a medium that offers less of an invitation by the individual to interact with others, but more of a cathartic release or self-presentation that often invites very little to no interaction, blogging. People can create a cyberself across many

DOI: 10.1057/9781137483416.0007

different media, one of which is a *blog*. This is akin to an online diary or ongoing report about one's life or a certain topic. In line with a number of the online behaviours outlined thus far in this text, work has been carried out to suggest an underlying social motivation to blogging behaviours (e.g., Chiang, Chiang & Lin, 2013). Chiang et al. (2013) consider the way in which early blogging behaviour was most associated with a more or less unidirectional commentary on the blogger's topic of choice. Blogging has now developed in so much to enable people to provide feedback or comment on a blog if the blogger activates such a function. This feedback could create in the blogger a sense of acceptance or belongingness, but could equally have negative consequences if the feedback is of a negative nature. Blogging might also be used as a mood management tool. If a blogger receives positive comments, then s/he might experience higher levels of positive mood. Equally, negative comments could serve to reinforce a negative mood. In line with this notion, Leung (2007) observed that some online behaviours and interactions, such as relationship maintenance, provided a temporary reduction in reported levels of offline stress. People may thus use blogging on the Internet to offset emotions and feelings currently being experienced in the offline world (e.g., Zillman, 1982; Zillman & Bryant, 1995).

Chen (2012) suggested that there is likely a predominant need that leads people to blog and proposed the action of blogging to help people meet the three human needs of *self-disclosure, affiliation* which is akin to a need for belonging and *achievement,* which is similar to goal-attainment. In a study that had 312 participants aged between 18 and 74 years complete an online survey style questionnaire, Chen (2012) found that their women participants were meeting a need to self-disclose and express their own voice in a way that leads to affiliation. Unfortunately, there is no report of the material that the female participants felt the need to discuss in these blogs. It would be of interest to ascertain whether their blogging behaviour and blog content is consistent with their actual self, or if they were using blogs to explore different versions of the self. Nonetheless, Chen offers evidence to suggest that self-presentation via blogs is of a goal-directed nature, with the three possible goals leading to the ultimate goal of psychological well-being. Another way in which online self-presentation may serve to enhance offline psychological well-being is through support-seeking behaviour online.

DOI: 10.1057/9781137483416.0007

5.12 The healthy (un)supporting Internet

There are as many reasons as to why people join support groups both online and offline as there are diverse groups to join. There is a growing literature on the two faces of the Internet: the ugly face of nefarious information and support arenas aimed at reaffirming one's negative self to the point of harm to the self. Such websites include those that promote eating disorders, suicide and self-harming. They are designed to entice people who are already experiencing distress and psychological upset in their offline lives, people who feel that they have no one to turn to offline. Online, it is easier to find groups of people who share in this negative self-concept. Under the guise of perceived anonymity, people can trawl the Internet to find acceptance for almost any aspect of human behaviour, positive, negative or even illegal. Such websites are designed to reel people in. Once some level of time and emotion has been invested, people find it more difficult to extricate themselves from such websites, forums and/or groups. This dark side of the web causes great concern for many government bodies, support agencies, charities and educational institutions, to name but a few, because it provides a self-reaffirming service to individuals. Given the wide-ranging concerns that result from such websites, it is unsurprising that we hear more about these in the mass media than those websites which are useful to individuals and which provide a positive recreation and reinforcement of peoples' self-concepts online. These provide the positive face of the Internet and can range from websites which promote psychological health and well-being for people who are experiencing psychological turmoil offline to those which are simple but efficient information portals. This section will consider some of the health benefits and deficits associated with joining online groups and seeking support online.

There are some new classic studies which suggest that focusing one's social efforts on interacting online could result in heighted levels of loneliness, depression and other anxiety related disorders. Kraut, Patterson, Lundmark, Kiesler, Mukhopadhyay and Scherlis (1998), for example, carried out the *HomeNet Project*. Over a period of two years, they tracked the use and psychological well-being of 73 homes which were given the Internet for the first time. Although there are a number of methodological issues associated with the study, this was one of the first demonstrations of a negative psychological impact of the Internet on peoples' offline selves. Kraut, Kiesler, Boneva, Cummings,

DOI: 10.1057/9781137483416.0007

Helgeson and Crawford (2002) did also carry out two follow up studies in which they clarify and qualify some of their findings, but of interest for the current text is that Kraut and colleagues in all of their studies demonstrate the chicken and egg dilemma of the Internet. That is, does information and support seeking along with online interaction affect individuals' self-construct, or is it the self-construct itself which directs people to use the Internet in a certain way. This question has largely been addressed in Chapter 3 of this text, but it should be noted here that there is probably no definitive answer to this question. Rather, it is likely an interaction of people seeking out personality-consistent behaviours online which, in turn, reinforce their personality. Iacovelli and Johnson (2012) reported the reduced likeability and social responsiveness of people who excessively used the Internet. There is a growing body of work that suggests that Internet overuse can lead to negative psychological symptoms, such as feeling lonely, stressed or depressed (e.g., Nie, Hillygus & Erbring, 2002). In the worst case scenario, people who have a negative self-image or low self-esteem may seek to reaffirm these negative affects through selective Internet use. This could lead to negative social comparisons of the individual feeling that they shall never attain the positive well-being displayed by those to whom they are comparing the self, and thus falling deeper into their negative psychological state. This would suggest a clear impact of online behaviours on the offline self.

Oftentimes, psychology becomes somewhat focused on the negatives of human behaviour, as has just occurred in this section. The Internet also offers an array of positive support, informational and motivational arenas for just about every positive human action conceivable. For example, if you are a keen runner you might belong to the Run England group, or the specific website of your local running club. These sites might provide you with positivism and motivation at times of self-doubt in your running ability. The Internet is also awash with all varieties of self-help advice, some of which may be of a charlatan nature, but a lot of which provides support and help in peoples' darkest hours. Indeed, online counselling and support is one of the fastest growing areas of Internet activity that falls under the umbrella term of E-health. E-health resources refer to "tools that enable consumers, patients, and informal caregivers to gather information, make health care decisions, communicate with health care providers, manage chronic disease, and engage in other health-related activities" (Lefebvre, Tada, Hilfiker & Baur, 2010, p. 667).

DOI: 10.1057/9781137483416.0007

In life, people often experience stressful or traumatic events which create enormous emotional responses that they initially find difficult to deal or cope with. Through information exchange via the Internet, they may however learn coping strategies that eventually lead to the acceptance of the event and any associated emotions or feelings. These are extended and complicated processes, the outlining of which is beyond the scope of this book. These processes do however influence the individual's view of self and how s/he subsequently fits in his/her offline world. The process of acceptance is often considered to be functional, a process of integrating the event-related information into memory for the self in a way that becomes less and less psychologically impactful to the individual (e.g., Foa & Kozak, 1986). Evidence that the Internet can be used to promote a more positive sense of self comes from Brody and Park (2004), who observed that the most psychological gain was observed when people communicate after a traumatic event via written communication. Iacovelli and Johnson (2012) offer an overview of some of the findings relating to online communications of thoughts, feelings and emotions after traumatic events via face-to-face compared to instant messaging modalities. They point out that online, people often feel that they can reveal aspects of the self that may not be socially acceptable offline in way that enables a freedom of expression not experienced offline for fear of negative social reactions and repercussions (e.g., Pennebaker & Harber, 1993). In line with the *stranger on the train phenomenon* (Rubin, 1975), often people share information in a one-off interaction, with no intent of ever interacting with that person again in the future (e.g., Bareket-Bojmel & Shahar, 2011). Thus, online support groups may provide an area to purge unwanted negative emotions and reinstate a positive sense of self in a way that avoids both the embarrassment and possible social rejection of a future interaction with a listener or respondent.

Finally, one might also wonder why people create the websites that offer advice, help and support. No doubt, there are a number of charities and agencies who create an online presence out of a sense of duty or as part of their ongoing commitment to help people. There are however an array of individuals who spend hours online offering help, support and advice. Joinson (2003) suggests that the purpose of online social support is to provide empathy, advice and support to people who have little in common other than a need for support or a willingness to supply support. It may be the case that the support provider engages in this behaviour as a cathartic release of their own inner turmoil (e.g., Preece, 2000)

DOI: 10.1057/9781137483416.0007

or simply to create the sense of belonging and feeling needed that they might require after experiencing their own negative offline events. One reason for taking on the role of the supporter/information provider in these situations might be to use the online forum as a *coping mechanism*, an aid to reinstating their own positive sense of psychological self and well-being (e.g., Pennebaker, 1989).

5.13   Concluding comments

This chapter has covered a snippet of social and social cognitive factors that play a role in shaping how people self-present online. The underlying theme of this chapter, and indeed of the entire text, is the notion of a flexible, malleable self-construct that can be selectively presented depending upon the Internet arena and goals sought of that presentation. Guided by internal and external factors, it would be unwise to suggest that any single factor is more or less important in whether people choose to present any given self on any specific website at any given time. The self is a flexible and malleable construct both online and offline, the presentation of which may be constrained by many different boundaries, including those set out between the producer and consumer of online content, and those established through societal norms and regulations of acceptable behaviour, both online and offline.

Across the five chapters of this book, a number of theories have been outlined, ranging from the purely personality and social psychological theories, to those of a social cognitive nature, to considering a uses and gratifications approach to understanding the Internet from a goal-directed perspective. On drawing all of this work together, it would appear that people are able to selectively present whichever aspect of the self online that serves to achieve a current behavioural or psychological goal. In doing so, they may use self-disclosure and other facets of human behaviour to present a version of self that will help attain that goal. While conveying this message, the book has also outlined a number of areas of future research across all of the chapters that provide an exciting and new approach to understanding how people create, edit and present themselves on the ever-evolving landscape that is the Internet.

DOI: 10.1057/9781137483416.0007

References

Adler, P. S., & Kwon, S.-W. (2002). Social capital: Prospects for a new concept. *Academy of Management Review, 27*(1), 17–40.

Agger, B. (2004). *The virtual self: A contemporary sociology.* Malden, MA; Oxford: Blackwell.

Alipoor, S., Goodarzi, A. M., Nezhad, M. Z., & Zaheri, L. (2009). Analysis of the relationship between physical self-concept and body image dissatisfaction in female students. *Social Sciences, 5*(1), 60–66.

Altman, I., & Taylor, D. (1973). *Social penetration: The development of interpersonal relationships.* New York: Holt, Rinehart & Winston.

Amichai-Hamburger, Y., & Vinitzky, G. (2010). Social network use and personality. *Computers in Human Behavior, 26*, 1289–1295.

Antheunis, M. L., & Schouten, A. P. (2011). The effects of other-generated and system-generated cues on adolescents' perceived attractiveness on social network sites. *Journal of Computer-Mediated Communication, 16*, 391–406.

Arkin, R. M. (1981). Self-presentational styles. In J. T. Tedeschi (ed.), *Impression management theory and social psychological research* (pp. 311–333). New York: Academic Press.

Attrill, A. (2012a). Self-disclosure online. In *Encyclopedia of Cyber Behavior.* Ing publishers: New York.

_____. (2012b). Sharing only parts of me: Categorical self-disclosure across Internet Arenas. *International Journal of Internet Science, 7*(1), 55–77.

_____. (2015). *Cyberpsychology*. Oxford, UK: Oxford University Press.

Attrill, A., & Jalil, R. (2011). Revealing only the superficial me: Exploring categorical self-disclosure online. *Computers in Human Behavior, 27*, 1634–1642.

Aykut Ceyhan, A., & Ceyhan, E. (2008). *CyberPsychology & Behavior, 11*(6), 699–701.

Back, M. D., Stopfer, J. M., Vazire, S., Gaddis, S., Schmukle, S. C., Egloff, B., & Gosling, S. D. (2010). Facebook profiles reflect actual personality, not self-idealisation. *Psychological Science, 21*(3), 372–374.

Bailenson, J. N., & Beall, A. C. (2006). Transformed social interaction: Exploring the digital plasticity of avatars. In R. Schroeder & A. Axelsson (eds.), *Avatars at work and play: Collaboration and interaction in shared virtual environments* (pp. 1–16). Springer-Verlag.

Bainbridge, W. S. (2010). *The warcraft civilisation: Social science in a virtual World*. Cambridge, MA: MIT Press.

Barack, A., & Gluck-Ofri, O. (2007). Degree and reciprocity of self-disclosure in online forums. *Cyberpsychology & Behavior, 10*(3), 407–417.

Bareket-Bojmel, L., & Shahar, G. (2011). Emotional and interpersonal consequences of self disclosure in a lived, online interaction. *Journal of Social and Clinical Psychology, 30*, 732–760.

Bargh, J. A., McKenna, K. Y. A., & Fitzsimons, G. M. (2002). Can you see the real me? Activation and expression of the "True Self" on the Internet. *Journal of Social Issues, 58*(1), 33–48.

Baumeister, R. F. (ed.) (1999). *The Self in Social Psychology*. Philadelphia, PA: Psychology Press (Taylor & Francis).

Baumeister, R. F., & Leary, M. R. (1995). The need to belong: Desire for interpersonal attachments as a fundamental human motivation. *Psychological Bulletin, 117*(3), 497–529.

Bellah, R. N., Madsen, R., Sullivan, W. M., Swidler, A., & Tipton, S. M. (1985). *Habits of the heart: Individualism and commitment in American life*. Berkeley: University of California Press.

Bem, D. J. (1972). Self-perception theory. In L. Berkowitz (ed.), *Advances in experimental social psychology, 6* (pp. 1–62). New York: Academic Press.

Ben-Ze'ev, A. (2005). "Detachment": The unique nature of online romantic relationships. In Y. Amichai-Hamburger (ed.), *The social net: Human behaviour in cyberspace* (pp. 116–138). New York: Oxford University Press.

DOI: 10.1057/9781137483416.0008

Berkowitz, L., & LePage, A. (1967). Weapons as aggression-eliciting stimuli. *Journal of Personality and Social Psychology, 7,* 202–207.

Berzonsky, M. D. (2003a). Identity style and well-being: Does commitment matter? *Identity, 3*(2), 131–142.

_____. (2003b). The structure of identity: Commentary on Jane Kroger's view of identity status transition. *Identity, 3*(3), 231–245.

Bettencourt, B. A., & Sheldon, K. (2001). Social roles as mechanisms for psychological need satisfaction within social groups. *Journal of Personality and Social Psychology, 81,* 1131–1143.

Bibby, P. A. (2008). Dispositional factors in the use of social networking sites: Findings and implications for social computing research. *Lecture Notes in Computer Science, 5075,* 392–400.

Boellstorff, T. (2008). *Coming of age in second life: An anthropologist explores the virtually human.* Princeton, NJ: Princeton University Press.

Bonebrake, K. (2002). College students' Internet use, relationship formation, and personality correlates. *Cyberpsychology & Behavior, 5,* 551–557.

Bowlby, J. (1969). *Attachment and Loss: Vol. 1. Attachment.* New York: Basic Books.

_____. (1973). *Attachment and Loss: Vol. 2. Separation Anxiety and Anger.* New York: Basic Books.

Boyd, D. M., & Ellison, N. B. (2007). Social network sites: Definition, history, and scholarship. *Journal of Computer-Mediated Communication, 13*(1), 210–230.

Brody, L., & Park, S. (2004). Narratives, mindfulness, and the implicit audience. *Clinical Psychology: Science and Practice, 11,* 147–154.

Brown, J. D. (2007). *The self.* New York: Psychology Press.

Campbell, J., Trapnell, P., Heine, S. J., Katz, I. M., Lavallee, L. R., & Lehman, D. R. (1996). Self-concept clarity: Measurement, personality correlates, and cultural boundaries. *Journal of Personality and Social Psychology, 70,* 141–156.

Carver, C. S., & Scheier, M. F. (1981). *Attention and self-regulation.* New York: Springer-Verlag.

_____. (1998). *On the self-regulation of behavior.* New York: Cambridge University Press.

Caspi, A., & Gorsky, P. (2006). Online deception: Prevalence, motivation, and emotion. *Cyberpsychology & Behavior, 9,* 54–59.

Castronova, E. (2005). *Synthetic worlds: The business and culture of online games.* Chicago: University of Chicago Press.

DOI: 10.1057/9781137483416.0008

Chelune, J.G. (1979). Measuring openness in interpersonal communication. In J. G. Chelune (ed.), *Self-disclosure: Origins, patterns and implications of openness in interpersonal relationships* (pp. 14–30). San Francisco, CA: Jossey-Bass.

Chen, B., & Markus, J. (2012). Students' self-presentation on Facebook: An examination of personality and self-construal factors. *Computers in Human Behavior, 28*, 2091–2099.

Chen, G. M. (2012). Why do women write personal blogs? Satisfying needs for self-disclosure and affiliation tell part of the story. *Computers in Human Behavior, 28*, 171–180.

Chester, A., & Bretherton, D. (2007). Impression management and identity online. In A. Joinson, K. McKenna, T. Postmes, & U. Reips (eds.), *The Oxford handbook of Internet Psychology* (pp. 223–236). Oxford: Oxford University Press.

Chiang, I.-P., Chiang, Y.-H., & Lin, Y.-C. L. (2013). The antecedents and consequences of blogging behaviour. *Social Behavior and Personality, 41*(2), 311–318.

Christofides, E., Muise, A., & Desmarais, S. (2009). Information disclosure and control on Facebook: Are they two sides of the same coin or two different processes. *CyberPsychology & Behavior, 12*, 341–345.

Claridge, T. (2004). *Social capital and natural resource management.* Brisbane, Australia: University of Queensland.

Clifton, A. (2014). Variability in personality expression across contexts: A social network approach. *Journal of Personality, 92*, 2.

Connelly, B. S., & Ones, D. S. (2010). An other perspective on personality: Meta-analytical integration of observers' accuracy and predictive validity. *Psychological Bulletin, 136*(6), 1092–1122.

Connolly, J. J., Kavanagh, E. J., & Viswesvaran, C. (2007). The convergent validity between self and observer ratings of personality: A meta-analytic review. *International Journal of Selection and Assessment, 15*(1), 110–117.

Conway, M. A., & Pleydell-Pearce, C. W. (2000). The construction of autobiographical memories in the self-memory system. *Psychological Review, 107*(2), 261–288.

Cooley, C. H. (1902). *Human nature and the social order.* New York: Scribner's.

Cooper, A., & Sportolari, L. (1997). Romance in cyberspace: Understanding online attraction. *Journal of Sex Education and Therapy, 22*, 7–14.

DOI: 10.1057/9781137483416.0008

Correa, T., Hinsley, A. W., & Gil de Zuniga, H. (2010). Who interacts on the Web?: The intersection of users' personality and social media use. *Computers in Human Behavior, 26*(2), 247–253.

Csikszentmihalyi, M. (1975). *Beyond boredom and anxiety.* San Francisco, CA: Jossey-Bass.

Davis, K. (2012). Friendship 2.0: Adolescents' experiences of belonging and self-disclosure online. *Journal of Adolescence, 35,* 1527–1536.

Davis, M. H., & Kraus, L. A. (1989). Social contact, loneliness, and mass media use: A test of two hypotheses. *Journal of Applied Social Psychology, 19,* 1100–1124.

DeAndrea, D. C. (2014). Advancing warranting theory. *Communication Theory, 24,* 186–204.

Deci. E. L., & Ryan, R. M. (2000). The "what" and "why" of goal pursuits: Human needs and the self-determination of behaviour. *Psychological Inquiry, 11*(4), 227–268.

DeHaan, S., Kuper, L. E., Magee, J. C., Bigelow, L. & Mustanski, B. S. (2013). The interplay between online and offline explorations of identity, relationships and sex: A mixed-methods study with LGBT youth. *Journal of Sex Research, 50*(5), 421–434.

Dinev, T., & Hart, P. (2006). An extended privacy calculus model for e-commerce transactions. *European Journal of Information Systems, 17*(1), 61–80.

Donne, J. (1572–1631). *Devotions upon emergent occasions and seuerall steps in my sicknes – Meditation XVII,* 1624.

Dunn, R. A., & Guadagno, R. E. (2012). My avatar and me – Gender and personality predictors of avatar-self discrepancy. *Computers in Human Behavior, 28,* 97–106.

Ellison, N., Heino, R., & Gibbs, J. (2006). Managing impressions online: Self-presentation processes in the online dating environment. *Journal of Computer-Mediated Communication, 11,* 415–441.

Evans, S. (2012). Virtual selves, real relationships: An exploration of the content and role for social interactions in the emergence of self in virtual environments. *Integrative Psychological and Behavioural Science, 46,* 512–528.

Eysenck, H. J., & Eysenck, M. W. (1985). *Personality and individual differences: A natural science approach.* New York: Plenum.

Festinger, L. (1954). A theory of social comparison processes. *Human Relations, 7*(2), 117–140.

DOI: 10.1057/9781137483416.0008

Foa, E., & Kozak, M. (1986). Emotional processing of fear: Exposure to corrective information. *Psychological Bulletin, 99*, 20–35.

Forest, A. L., & Wood, J. V. (2012). When social networking is not working: Individuals with low self-esteem recognize but do not repeat the benefits of self-disclosure on Facebook. *Psychological Science, 23,* 295–302.

Fullwood, C. (2015). The role of personality in online self-presentation. In A. Attrill (ed.), *Cyberpsychology.* Oxford: Oxford University Press.

Gibbs, J. L., Ellison, N. B., & Heino, R. D. (2006). Self-presentation in online personals: The role of anticipated future interaction, self-disclosure, and perceived success in internet dating. *Communication Research, 33*(2), 152–177.

Gibbs, J. L., Ellison, N. B., & Lai, C. (2011). First comes love, then comes Google: An investigation of uncertainty reduction strategies and self-disclosure in online dating. *Communication Research, 38,* 70–100.

Giles, H., Coupland, N., & Coupland, J. (1991). *Accommodation theory: Communication, context, and consequence.* New York: Cambridge University Press.

Gill, A. J., Oberlander, J., & Austin, E. (2006). Rating e-mail personality at zero acquaintance. *Personality and Individual Differences, 40*(3), 497–507.

Goffman, E. (1959). *The presentation of self in everyday life.* Garden City: Doubleday-Anchor.

_____. (1983). The interaction order: American sociological association, 1982 presidential address. *American Sociological Review, 48*(1), 1–17.

Gonzales, A. L., & Hancock, J. T. (2011). Mirror, mirror on my Facebook wall: Effects of exposure to Facebook on self-esteem. *Cyberpsychology, Behavior, and Social Networking, 14,* 79–83.

Gosling, S. D., Augustine, A. A., Vazire, S., Holtzman, N., & Gaddis, S. (2011). Manifestations of personality in online social networks: Self-reported Facebook-related behaviors and observable profile information. *Cyberpsychology, Behavior and Social Networking, 14*(9), 483–488.

Gosling, S.D., Gaddis, S., & Vazire, S. (2007). Personality impressions based on Facebook profiles. In *Proceedings of the international conference on weblogs and social media* (pp. 26–28). CA: AAAI Boulder, CO. Menlo Park.

Granovetter, M. (1982). The strength of weak ties: A network theory revisited. In P. Marsden & N. Lin (eds.), *Social structure and network analysis.* Beverly Hills, CA: Sage.

DOI: 10.1057/9781137483416.0008

Greene, K., Derlega, V. L., & Mathews, A. (2006). Self-disclosure in personal relationships. In A.Vangelisti & D. Perlman (eds.), *Cambridge handbook of personal relationships* (pp. 1268–1328). Cambridge, UK: Cambridge University Press.

Hampton, K., Goulet, L. S., Rainie, L., & Purcell, K. (2011, June 16). Social networking sites and our lives: How people's trust, personal relationships, and civic and political involvements are connected to their use of social networking sites and other technologies. *Pew Internet and American Life Project.* Retrieved from http://www.pewinternet.org/Reports/2011/Technology-and-social-networks.aspx.

Harter, S. (1998). *The development of self-representations.* New York: Wiley.

Heeter, C. (1992). Being there: The subjective experience of presence. *Presence, 1*(2), 262–271.

Heider, F. (1958). *The psychology of interpersonal relations.* New York: Wiley.

Hew, K. F. (2011). Students' and teachers' use of Facebook. *Computers in Human Behavior, 27,* 662–676.

Higgins, E. T. (1987). Self-discrepancy: A theory relating self and affect. *Psychological Review, 94,* 319–340.

_____. (1997). Beyond pleasure and pain. *American Psychologist, 52*(12), 1290–1300.

Hillier, L., & Harrison, L. (2007). Building realities less limited than their own: Young people practicing same-sex attraction on the Internet. *Sexualities, 10,* 82–100.

Hofstede, G. (1980). *Culture consequences: International differences in work-related values.* Beverly Hills, CA: Sage.

Hogan, B. (2010). The presentation of self in the age of social media: Distinguishing performances and exhibitions online. *Bulletin of Science, Technology & Society, 30*(6), 377–386.

Iacovelli, A. M., & Johnson, C. (2012). Disclosure through face-to-face and instant messaging modalities: Psychological and physiological effects. *Journal of Social and Clinical Psychology, 31*(3), 225–250.

James, W. (1890). *The principles of psychology.* New York: Holt.

Joinson, A. N. (2001). Knowing me, knowing you: Reciprocal self-disclosure on the Internet. *Cyberpsychology & Behavior, 4*(5), 587–591.

_____. (2003). *Understanding the psychology of internet behavior.* Hampshire: Palgrave Macmillan.

DOI: 10.1057/9781137483416.0008

Joinson, A. N., Reips, U.-D., Buchanan, T., & Paine-Schofield, C. B. (2010). Privacy, trust, and self-disclosure online. *Human-Computer Interaction, 25*, 1–24.

Jourard, S. M. (1971). *The transparent self* (2nd ed.). New York: Van Nostrand Reinhold.

Kahn, J. H., & Hessling, R. M. (2001). Measuring the tendency to conceal versus disclose psychological distress. *Journal of Social and Clinical Psychology, 20*, 40–65.

Katz, E., Blumler, J. G., & Gurevitch, M. (1973). Uses and gratifications research. *Public Opinion Quarterly, 37*(4), 509–523.

Kelley, H. H. (1967). Attribution theory in social psychology. *Nebraska Symposium on Motivation, 15*, 192–238.

Kernis, M. H., & Goldman, B. M. (2006). A multi-component conceptualization of authenticity: Theory and research. In M. P. Zanna (ed.), *Advances in experimental social psychology* (pp. 283–387). New York: Academic Press.

Kim, J., LaRose, R., & Wei, P. (2009). Loneliness as the cause and the effect of problematic internet use: The relationship between internet use and psychological well-being. *CyberPsychology & Behavior, 12*(4): 451–455.

Kim, Y., & Sundar. S. S. (2012). Visualizing ideal self vs. actual self through avatars: Impact on Preventive health outcomes. *Computers in Human Behavior, 28*, 1356–1364.

Koroleva, K., Brecht, F., Goebel, L., & Malinova, M. (2011). "Generation Facebook" – A cognitive calculus model of teenage user behaviour on social network sites. In *Proc AMCIS* 2011, Detroit.

Kraut, R., Kiesler, S., Boneva, B., Cummings, J., Helgeson, V., & Crawford, A. (2002). Internet paradox revisited. *Journal of Social Issues, 58*(1), 49–74.

Kraut, R. E., Patterson, M., Lundmark, V., Kiesler, S., Mukhopadhyay, T., & Scherlis, W. (1998). Internet paradox: A social technology that reduces social involvement and psychological well-being? *American Psychologist, 53*(9), 1017–1032.

Lakey, C. E., Kernis, M. H., Heppner, W. L., & Lance, C. E. (2008). Individual differences in authenticity and mindfulness as predictors of verbal defensiveness. *Journal of Research in Personality, 42*, 230–238.

LaRose, R., Eastin, M. S., & Gregg, J. (2001). Reformulating the Internet paradox: Social cognitive explanations of Internet use and depression. *Journal of Online Behavior, 1*(2). Retrieved from

DOI: 10.1057/9781137483416.0008

http://s3.amazonaws.com/lcp/sinergiaymente/myfiles/Depression-Journal.htm on 7 January 2015.

Larson, D. G., & Chastain, R. L. (1990). Self-concealment: Conceptualization, measurement, and health implications. *Journal of Social and Clinical Psychology, 9*, 439–455.

Leary, M. R. (1995). *Self-presentation, impression management and interpersonal behaviour*. Madison, WI: Brown and Benchmark.

Leary, M. R. & Allen, A. B. (2011). Personality and persona: Personality processes in self-presentation. *Journal of Personality, 79*(6), 889–916.

Lee, B. W., & Stapinski, L. A. (2011). Seeking safety on the internet: Relationship between social anxiety and problematic internet use. *Journal of Anxiety Disorders, 26*(1), 197–205.

Lee, C., Aiken, K. D., Hung, H. C. (2012). Effects of college students' video gaming behaviour on self-concept clarity and flow. *Social Behavior and Personality, 40*(4), 673–680.

Lee, J.-E. R., Moore, D. C., Park, E.-A., & Park, S. G. (2012). Who wants to be "friendrich"? Social compensatory friending on Facebook and the moderating role of public self-consciousness. *Computers in Human Behavior, 28*, 1036–1043.

Lee, K. M. (2004). Presence, explicated. *Communication Theory, 14*(1), 27–50.

Lefebvre, R. C., Tada, T., Hilfiker, S. W., & Baur, C. (2010). The assessment of user engagement with eHealth content: The eHealth engagement scale. *Journal of Computer-Mediated Communication, 15*(4), 666–681.

Leung, L. (2002). Loneliness, self-disclosure, and ICQ ("I Seek You") use. *CyberPsychology & Behavior. 5*, 241–251.

_____. (2007). Stressful life events, motives for Internet use, and social support among digital kids. *Cyberpsychology & Behavior, 10*(2), 204–214.

Liao, C. (2011). Virtual fashion play as embodied identity re/assembling: Second life fashion bloggers and their avatar bodies. In A. Peachey & M. Childs (eds.), *Reinventing ourselves: Contemporary concepts of identity in virtual Worlds* (pp. 101–127). London: Springer.

Lin, N. (2002). *Social capital: A theory of social structure and action*. Cambridge University Press.

Luyckx, K., Schwartz, S. J., Goossens, L., Soenens, B., & Beyers, W. (2008). Developmental typologies of identity formation and adjustment in female emerging adults: A latent class growth analysis

DOI: 10.1057/9781137483416.0008

approach. *Journal of Research on Adolescence (Blackwell Publishing Limited), 18*(4), 595–619.

Maghrabi, R.O., Oakley, R.L., & Nemati, H.R. (2014). The impact of self-selected identity on productive or perverse social capital in social network sites. *Computers in Human Behavior, 33*, 367–371.

Magno, C. (2009). The development of the self-disclosure scale. In C. Magno & J. Ouano (eds.), *Designing written assessment for student learning*. Manilla, NSW: Phoenix Pub.

Malhotra, N. K., Kim, S. S., & Agarwal, J. (2004). Internet users' information privacy concerns (IUIPC): The construct, the scale, and a causal model. *Information Systems Research, 15*(4), 336–355.

Marcia, J. E. (1993). The status of the statuses: Research review. In J. Marcia, A.Waterman, D. Matteson, S. Archer, & J. Orlofsky (eds.), *Ego identity* (pp. 22–41). New York: Springer-Verlag.

Marcus, B., Machilek, F., & Schutz, A. (2006). Personality in cyberspace: Personal web sites as media for personality expressions and impressions. *Journal of Personality and Social Psychology, 90*(6), 1014–1031.

Markus, H. R., & Kitayama, S. (1991). Culture and the self: Implications for cognition, emotion and motivation. *Psychological Review, 98*(2), 224–253.

Markus, H., & Nurius, P. (1986). Possible selves. *American Psychologist, 41*(9), 954–956.

Marriott, T. C., & Buchanan, T. (2014). The true self online: Personality correlates of preference for self-expression online, and observer ratings of personality online and offline. *Computers in Human Behavior, 32*, 171–177.

Maslow, A. H. (1943). A theory of human motivation. *Psychological Review, 50*, 370–396.

McCarthey, S. J., & Moje, E. B. (2002). Identity Matters. *Reading Research, Quarterly, 37*(2), 228–238.

McCrae, R., & Costa, Jr. P. (1987). Validation of the five-factor model of personality across instruments and observers. *Journal of Personality and Social Psychology, 52*(1), 81–90.

McIntosh, W. D., & Martin, L. L. (1992). The cybernetics of happiness: The relation between goal attainment, rumination, and affect. In M. S. Clark (ed.), *Review of personality and social psychology, 14*, 222–246. Newbury Park, CA: Sage.

McKenna, K. Y. A., & Bargh, J. A. (1998). Coming out in the age of the Internet: Identity de-marginalization from virtual group

DOI: 10.1057/9781137483416.0008

participation. *Journal of Personality and Social Psychology, 74* (September).

McKenna, K. Y. A., Green, A. S., & Gleason, M. E. J. (2002). Relationship formation on the internet: What's the big attraction? *Journal of Social Issues, 58*(1), 9–31.

Mead, G. H. (1956). *The social psychology of George Herbet Mead.* Chicago: University of Chicago Press.

Meeus, W. (1996). Studies on identity development in adolescence: An overview of research and some new data. *Journal of Youth and Adolescence, 25*(5), 569–598.

Meeus, W., Iedema, J., Helsen, M., & Vollebergh, W. (1999). Patterns of adolescent identity development: Review of literature and longitudinal analysis. *Developmental Review, 19*(4), 419–461.

Metzger, M. J. (2004). Privacy, trust, and disclosure: Exploring barriers to electronic commerce. *Journal of Computer-Mediated Communication, 9*(4).

Meyrowitz, J. (1989). The generalized elsewhere. *Critical Studies of Mass Communication, 6*(3), 323–334.

Moon, Y. (2000). Intimate exchanges: Using computers to elicit self-disclosure from consumers. *Journal of Consumer Research, 26*, 323–339.

Mustanski, B., Newcomb, M., & Garofalo, R. (2011). Mental health of lesbian, gay, and bisexual youth: A developmental resiliency perspective. *Journal of Gay and Lesbian Social Services, 23*, 204–225.

Myddleton, J. & Attrill, A. (2015). Online relationships. In A. Attrill (ed.), *Cyberpsychology*, Oxford University Press, UK: Oxford.

Myers, P. N., & Biocca, F. A. (1992). The elastic body image: The effect of television advertising and programming on body image distortions in young women. *Journal of Communication, 42*(3), 108–133.

Nadkarni, A., & Hofmann, S. G. (2012). Why do people use Facebook? *Personality and Individual Differences, 52*, 243–249.

Nardi, B. A. (1996). Studying context: A comparison of activity theory, situated action models and distributed cognition. In B. A. Nardi (ed.), *Context and consciousness: Activity theory and human computer interaction* (pp. 69–101). Cambridge, MA: MIT Press.

Nguyen, M., Bin, Y. S., & Campbell, A. (2012). Comparing online and offline self-disclosure: A systematic review. *Cyberpsychology Behavior and Social Networking, 15*(2), 103–111.

Nie, N. H., Hillygus, D. S., & Erbing, L. (2002). Internet use, interpersonal relationships, and sociability: A time diary study. In

DOI: 10.1057/9781137483416.0008

B. Wellman & C. Haythornthwaite (eds.), *The Internet in everyday life* (pp. 215–244). Oxford, England: Blackwell.

Novak, T., Hoffman, D., & Yung, Y.-F. (2000). Measuring the customer experience in online environments: A structural modeling approach. *Marketing Science, 19*, 22–42.

Odasz, F. (1991). *Big sky telegraph: Vision and summary. "Growing an Innovation Support Testbed"*. Retrieved from http://www.info-ren.org/projects/universal-service/local-resources/odasz_5.html on 9 January 2015.

Okdie, B. M., Guadagno, R. E., Bernieri, F. J., Geers, A. L., & Mclarney-Vesotski, A. R. (2011). Getting to know you: Face-to-face versus online interactions. *Computers in Human Behavior, 27*(1), 153–159.

Ortony, A., Clore, G. L., & Collings, A. (1988). *The cognitive structure of emotions*. Cambridge: Cambridge University Press.

Pak, M. (2014). The digital self: Boundaries and fusions. *Journal of Marketing Theory and Practice, 22*(2), 141–142.

Papacharissi, Z., & Mendelson, A. (2011). Toward a new(er) sociability: Uses, gratifications and social capital on Facebook. In S. Papathanassopoulos (ed.), *Media perspectives for the 21st century* (pp. 212–230). New York: Routledge.

Parks, M. R., & Floyd, K. (1986). Making friends in cyberspace. *Journal of Communication, 46*, 80–97.

Parks, M. R., & Roberts, L. D. (1998). "Making Moosic": The development of personal relationships online and a comparison to their off-line counterparts. *Journal of Social and Personal Relationships, 15*, 517–537.

Pennebaker, J., & Harber, K. (1993). A social stage model of collective coping: The Loma Prieta earthquake and the Persian Gulf War. *Journal of Social Issues, 49*, 125–145.

Pennebaker, J. W. (1989). Confession, inhibition, and disease. In L. Berkowitz (ed.), *Advances in experimental social psychology* (pp. 211–244). New York: Academic Press.

Pervin, L. A. (1993). *Personality* (6th ed.). Canada: Wiley.

Peter, J., Valkenburg, P. M., & Schouten, A. P. (2005). Developing a model of adolescent friendship formation on the internet. *Cyberpsychology & Behavior, 8*(5), 423–430.

Petronio, S. (2002). *Boundaries of privacy: Dialectics of disclosure*. Albany, NY: SUNY Press.

DOI: 10.1057/9781137483416.0008

_____. (2007). Translational research endeavors and the practices of communication privacy management. *Journal of Applied Communication Research, 35*(3), 218–222.

Petronio, S., & Bradford, L. (1993). Issues interfering with the use of written communication as a means of relational bonding between absentee, divorced fathers and their children. *Journal of Applied Communication Research, 21*(2), 163–175.

Petronio, S., & Durham, W. T. (2008). Communication privacy management theory. In L. A. Baxter & D. O. Braithewaite (eds.), *Engaging theories in interpersonal communication: Multiple perspectives* (pp. 309–322). Thousand Oaks, CA: Sage.

Petronio, S., Martin, J., & Littlefield, R. (1984). Prerequisite conditions for self-disclosing: A gender issue. *Communication Monographs, 51*(3), 268–273.

Portes, A. (1998). Social capital: Its origins and applications in modern sociology. *Annual Review of Sociology, 24*(1), 1–24.

Preece, J. (2000). *Online communities – designing usability, supporting sociability.* Chichester: Wiley.

Rai, R., & Attrill, A. (2014). *The effects of synchronous and asynchronous internet communication, personality, and representations of the self on the uptake of online video communication.* Poster presented at the 16th International Conference on Human Computer Interaction, Crete, June 2014.

Rollman, J. B., Krug, K., & Parente, F. (2000). The chat room phenomenon: Reciprocal communication in cyberspace. *CyberPsychology & Behavior, 3*, 161–166.

Rosen, D., Stefanone, M. A., & Lackaff, D. (2010, January). Online and offline social networks: Investigating culturally-specific behavior and satisfaction. In Proceedings of *IEEE's hawaii international conference on systems science (HICSS)*, Los Alamitos, CA: IEEE Press.

Rouse, S. V., & Haas, H. A. (2003). Exploring the accuracies and inaccuracies of personality perception following internet-mediated communication. *Journal of Research in Personality, 37*(5), 446–467.

Rubin, Z. (1975). Disclosing oneself to a stranger: Reciprocity and its limits. *Journal of Experimental Social Psychology, 11*, 233–260.

Rui, J., & Stefanone, M. A. (2013). Strategic self-presentation online: A cross-cultural study. *Computers in Human Behavior, 29*, 110–118.

Ryan, R. M., LaGuardia, J. G., & Rawsthorne, L. J. (2005). Self-complexity and the authenticity of self-aspects on well being and

DOI: 10.1057/9781137483416.0008

resilience to stressful events. *North American Journal of Psychology, 7,* 431–448.

Scharlott, B. W., & Christ, W. G. (1995). Overcoming relationship-initiation barriers: The impact of a computer-dating system on sex role, shyness, and appearance inhibitions. *Computers in Human Behavior, 11*(2), 191–204.

Schlegel, R. J., & Hicks, J. A. (2011). The true self and psychological health: Emerging evidence and future directions. *Personality and Social Psychology Compass, 5,* 989–1003.

Schlegel, R. J., Hicks, J. A., Arndt, J., & King. L. A. (2009). Thine own self: True self-concept accessibility and meaning in life. *Journal of Personality and Social Psychology, 96,* 473–490.

Schlegel, R.J., Vess, M., & Arndt, J. (2013). To discover or to create: Metaphors and the true self. *Journal of Personality, 80*(4), 969–993.

Schulman, S., Seiffge-Krenke, I., & Dimitrovsky, L. (1994). The functions of pen pals for adolescents. *Journal of Psychology: Interdisciplinary and Applied, 128*(1), 89–100.

Seibt, J., & Nørskov, M. (2012). "Embodying" the internet: Towards the moral self via communication robots? *Philosophy and Technology, 25,* 285–307.

Seidman, G. (2013). Self-presentation and belonging on Facebook: How personality influences social media use and motivations. *Personality and Individual Differences, 54,* 402–407.

Sheldon, K. M., Abad, N., & Hirsch, C. (2011). A two-process view of Facebook use and relatedness need-satisfaction: Disconnection drives use, and connection rewards it. *Journal of Personality and Social Psychology, 100,* 766–775.

Sheldon, K. M., Ryan, R. M., Rawsthorne, L., & Ilardi, B. (1997). "True" self and "trait" self: Cross-role variation in the Big Five traits and its relations with authenticity and well-being. *Journal of Personality and Social Psychology, 73,* 1380–1393.

Sheldon, P. (2008a). The relationship between unwillingness-to-communicate and students' Facebook use. *Journal of Media Psychology, 20,* 67–75.

_____. (2008b). Student favorite: Facebook and motives for its use. *Southwestern Mass Communication Journal, 23*(2), 39–53.

Smock, A. D. (2011). Facebook as a toolkit: A uses and gratification approach to unbundling feature use. *Computers in Human Behavior, 27*(8), 2322–2329.

DOI: 10.1057/9781137483416.0008

Special, W. P., & Li-Barber, K. T. (2012). Self-disclosure and student satisfaction with Facebook. *Computers in Human Behavior, 28,* 624–630.

Standage, T. (1998). *The Victorian internet: The remarkable story of the telegraph and the nineteenth century's on-line pioneers.* Bloomsbury, NY.

Steinfield, C., Ellison, N. B., & Lampe, C. (2008). Social capital, self-esteem, and use of online social network sites: A longitudinal analysis. *Journal of Applied Developmental Psychology, 29*(6), 434–445.

Sternberg, R.J. (1986). A triangular theory of love. *Psychological Review, 93,* 119–135.

Subrahmanyam, K., & Greenfield, P. (2008). Online communication and adolescent relationships. *The Future of Children, 18,* 119–146.

Taylor, T. L. (2002). Living digitally: Embodiment in virtual worlds. In R. Schroeder (ed.), *The social life of avatars: Presence and interaction in shared virtual environments* (pp. 40–62). London: Springer.

Ten Berge, M. A., & De Raad, B. (1999). Taxonomies of situations from a trait psychological perspective: A review. *European, Journal of Personality, 13,* 337–360.

Tesser, A., Millar, M., & Moore, J. (1988). Some affective consequences of social comparison and reflection processes: The pain and pleasure of being close. *Journal of Personality and Social Psychology, 54*(1), 49–61.

Tiggemann, M., & Mcgill, B. (2004). The role of social comparison in the effect of magazine advertisements on women's mood and body dissatisfaction. *Journal of Social and Clinical Psychology, 23*(1), 23–44.

Tiggemann, M., & Slater, A. (2004). Thin ideals in music television: A source of social comparison and body dissatisfaction. *International Journal of Eating Disorders, 35*(1), 48–58.

Ting-Toomey, S. (1999). *Communicating across cultures.* New York: Guilford Press.

Tosun, L. P. (2012). Motives for Facebook use and expressing "true self" on the internet. *Computers in Human Behavior, 28,* 1510–1517.

Tosun, L. P., & Lajunen, T. (2010). Does internet use reflect your personality? Relationship between Eysenck's personality dimensions and internet use. *Computers in Human Behavior, 26*(2), 162–167.

Triandis, H. C. (1994). *Culture and Social Behavior.* New York: McGraw-Hill.

Turkle, S. (1995). *Life on the screen: Identity in the age of the Internet.* New York, NY: Simon & Schuster.

DOI: 10.1057/9781137483416.0008

_____. (1997). *Life on the screen: Identity in the age of the internet.* London: Phoenix.

Utz, S. (2010). Show me your friends and I will tell you what type of person you are: How one's profile, number of friends, and type of friends influence impression formation on social network sites. *Journal of Computer-Mediated Communication, 15,* 314–335.

Uysal, A., Lin, H. L., & Knee, C. R. (2010). The role of need satisfaction in self-concealment and well-being. *Personality and Social Psychology Bulletin, 36*(2), 187–199.

Valkenburg, P. I., Schouten, A. P., & Peter, J. (2005). Adolescents' identity experiments on the internet. *New Media and Society, 7*(3), 383–402.

Valkenburg, P. M., & Peter, J. (2007). Preadolescents' and adolescents' online communication and their closeness to friends. *Developmental Psychology, 43*(2), 267–277.

Vasalou, A., Joinson, A., Bänziger, T., Goldie, P., & Pitt, J. (2008). Avatars in social media: Balancing accuracy, playfulness and embodied messages. *International Journal of Human–Computer Studies, 66*(11), 801–811.

Veerapen, M. (2011). Encountering oneself and the other: A case study of identity formation in Second Life. In A. Peachey & M. Childs (eds.), *Reinventing ourselves: Contemporary concepts of identity in virtual Worlds.* London: Springer.

Vygotsky, L. S. (1978). *Mind in society.* Cambridge, MA: Harvard University Press.

Walther, J. B. (1992). Interpersonal effects in computer-mediated interaction: A relational perspective. *Communication Research, 19,* 52–90.

_____. (1996). Computer-mediated communication: Impersonal, interpersonal, and hyperpersonal interaction. *Communication Research, 23,* 3–44.

_____. (2011).Theories of computer-mediated communication and interpersonal relations. In M. L. Knapp, & J. A. Daly (eds.), *The SAGE handbook of interpersonal communication* (4th ed., pp. 443–480). Thousand Oaks, CA: Sage.

Walther, J. B., & Parks, M. R. (2002). Cues filtered out, cues filtered in: Computer-mediated communication and relationships. In M. L. Knapp & J. A. Daly (eds.), *Handbook of interpersonal communication* (3rd ed., pp. 529–563). Thousand Oaks, CA: Sage.

DOI: 10.1057/9781137483416.0008

Walther, J. B., Van Der Heide, B., Hamel, L., & Schulman, H. (2009). Self-generated versus other-generated statements and impressions in computer-mediated communication: A test of warranting theory using Facebook. *Communication Research, 36,* 229–253.

Walther, J. B., Van Der Heide, B., Kim, S., Westerman, D., & Tong, S. T. (2008).The role of friends' behavior on evaluations of individuals' Facebook profiles: Are we known by the company we keep? *Human Communication Research, 34,* 28–49.

Wheeless, L. R. (1978). A follow-up study of the relationships among trust, disclosure, and interpersonal solidarity. *Human Communication Research, 4,* 143–157.

Wheeless, L. R., & Grotz, J. (1976). Conceptualization and measurement of reported self-disclosure. *Human Communication Research, 2,* 338–346.

Whitty, M., & Carr, A. (2006). *Cyberspace romance.* Basingstoke: Palgrave Macmillan.

Wilson, R. E., Gosling, S. D., & Graham, L. T. (2012). A review of Facebook research in the social sciences. *Perspectives on Psychological Science, 7*(3), 203–220.

Wood, A. M., Linley, P. A., Maltby, J., Baliousis, M., & Joseph, S. (2008). The authentic personality: A theoretical and empirical conceptualization and the development of the Authenticity Scale. *Journal of Counseling Psychology, 55,* 385–399.

Yamagishi, T. (2001). Trust as a form of social intelligence. In K. Cook (ed.), *Trust in Society* (pp. 121–147). New York: Russell Sage Foundation.

Yee, N., & Bailenson, J. (2007). The proteus effect: The effect of transformed self-representation on behaviour. *Human Communication Research, 33,* 271–290.

Yu, A. Y., Tian, S. W., Vogel, D., & Kwok, R. C.-W. (2010). Can learning be virtually boosted? An investigation of online social networking impacts. *Computers and Education, 55,* 1494–1503.

Yum, Y.-O., & Hara, K. (2006). Computer-mediated relationship development: A cross-cultural comparison. *Journal of Computer-Mediated Communication, 11,* 133–152.

Zhao, S., Grasmuck, S., & Martin, J. (2008). Identity construction on Facebook: Digital empowerment in anchored relationships. *Computers in Human Behavior, 24,* 1816–1836.

Zillman, D. (1982). Television viewing and arousal. In D. Pearl, L. Bouthilet, & J. Lazar (eds.), *Television and behaviour: Ten years of*

DOI: 10.1057/9781137483416.0008

scientific progress and implications for the eighties, Vol. 2, technical reviews (pp. 53–67). Washington, DC: Government printing Office.

Zillman, D., & Bryant, J. (1985). Affect, mood, and emotion as determinants of selective media exposure. In D. Zillman & J. Bryant (eds.), *Selective exposure to communication* (pp. 157–190). Hillsdale, NJ: Lawrence Erlbaum.

DOI: 10.1057/9781137483416.0008

Index

Lightning Source UK Ltd.
Milton Keynes UK
UKOW04n1828100315

247650UK00001B/22/P